Dedicated to the pupils of Thomas Becket
Upper School, Northampton and in memory
of the late Rev. Dr A. Marcus Ward,
Richmond and Heythrop Colleges,
University of London.

Contents

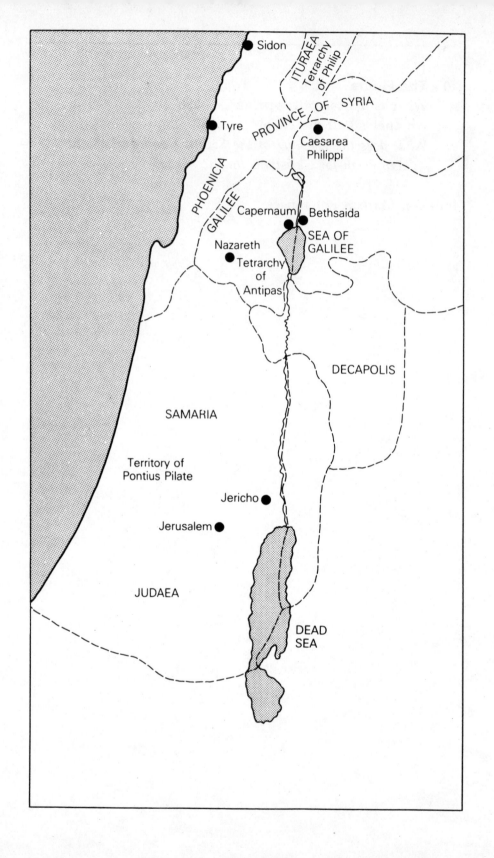

Preface

This book attempts to present the results of modern biblical scholarship, applied to Mark's Gospel at a suitable level for school students.

I have tried to simplify the ideas of scholarship, but at the same time, remain faithful to the views expressed therein.

Mark's Gospel is not a book for the casual reader, it is complex and needs interpretation, especially for students to understand both its original meaning and its modern day relevance.

I have written the book for the classroom, with special reference to those studying for GCSE examinations. The book covers the whole of Mark's Gospel, although certain parts of the Gospel are not required by some Examination Boards to be studied. I have tried to be simple in both language and structure. It has been my intention to encourage students to have an enquiring and critical approach to the Gospel, and to help students explore:

- the background against which the Gospel was written;
- the original ideas of the Gospel;
- the influence of both the early Church and the author on the traditions about Jesus; and
- the relevance of the Gospel for Christians today.

At various points, sometimes within and always at the end of each chapter, there are work sections. These follow the assessment objectives of the GCSE syllabus: knowledge, understanding and evaluation. In addition there are sections on practical work. Finally there are sections containing a 'stepped question' for examination practice.

All references quoted both from Mark's Gospel and other Biblical books are taken from the New English Bible. Mark quotes may be easily identified by this Logo

Sections which discuss Mark's Gospel 'for today' are in italics and are, therefore, easily identifiable throughout the book.

I would like to thank my colleagues, Miss Correna Dcaccia and Mr Vincent Love for their encouragement and advice; Mr Peter Chlubek for his technical assistance in preparing the typescript and Lucie, my wife, for all her help.

1 The Background to Mark's Gospel

For a hundred years or so before the birth of Jesus, Palestine had been under the rule of the Romans.

By the time Jesus began his ministry, the province of Judaea was governed by the Roman Governor, who was known as the Procurator. His name was Pontius Pilate. Herod Antipas, the son of Herod the Great, ruled over Galilee for the Romans. Under Roman occupation the Jews were allowed a good deal of self-administration.

The Religious Background at the Time of Jesus

Sanhedrin

The Sanhedrin was the highest court of Jewish law both religious and political. The name 'Sanhedrin' means 'council'. The president of the council was the high priest. The Sanhedrin dealt with all serious cases and was the final court. of appeal.

The origin of the Sanhedrin was the seventy men Moses appointed to assist him in judging the children of Israel. The seventy members of the Sanhedrin were drawn mainly from two opposing parties, the Sadducees and the Pharisees. In criminal cases the Sanhedrin could pass a sentence of death but could not carry out such a sentence without the approval of the Roman Procurator.

Pharisees

The Pharisees were far more influential among the people than the Sadducees. They were the progressive party of Judaism. For them religious life centred round the study and keeping of the Law of Moses. Their heritage can be traced back to the time of the destruction of the Temple in 586 BC, when the Jews were taken captive into exile by the Babylonians. All that the loyal Jew in exile had left to keep the faith alive was a strict keeping of the Law of Moses, contained in the Pentateuch. (The Pentateuch is the Law of

Moses found in the first five books of the Old Testament. It is sometimes called the Torah.)

In the second century BC, when Judah was occupied by the Greeks, the Pharisees were the ones who refused all Greek influences. They became known as the 'separated ones' (this is what the name Pharisee means) because of their refusal to compromise. Their aim was to keep alive the traditional Jewish faith.

WHAT THE PHARISEES BELIEVED

- The Pharisees wished to protect the Law and make it fit every need of daily life.
- They strictly upheld the oral law, which was developed by the Scribes to interpret the Law of Moses.
- In their desire to keep the Law, they surrounded it with:

  (a) a great many minute regulations;
  (b) volumes of explanations; and
  (c) all sorts of complicated additions.

- This 'oral law' was equally as binding as the written Law of Moses. It was later written down in two books called the *Mishnah* and the *Talmud*.
- The Pharisees looked forward to the coming of the Messiah.
- The Pharisees believed in a form of resurrection at the last day.

It is understandable that the Pharisees were opposed to Jesus for he criticised them for spending so much time keeping the letter of the Law that they had forgotten how to care for the needs of people (see chapter 6).

Sadducees

The Sadducees claimed direct descent from Zadok who was the High Priest at the time of King Solomon (1 Kings 2:35). The Sadducees were priests. They were the upper class in

Jewish society, living in ease and comfort. They had control of the Temple worship, sacrifices and finances. They were very conservative in their political outlook and wanted things to remain exactly as they were under the Romans. They were content, therefore, to work in co-operation with the Romans.

WHAT THE SADDUCEES BELIEVED

The beliefs of the Sadducees differed from other religious parties.

- They did not believe in the coming of the Messiah, especially the popular idea of the Messiah who would free the people from the Romans. This would lead to conflict with Rome and this had to be avoided at all costs.
- Their only rule of religious, moral and social life was the **Law of Moses** as found in the first five books of the Old Testament (called the **Pentateuch** or the **Torah**). They took the Commandments of Moses literally.
- They laid little emphasis on the message of the prophets.
- They refused to be bound by the **'Oral law'** which explained the written Law of Moses (see Scribes and Pharisees).
- They did not believe in any form of resurrection.

It is understandable that the Sadducees were opposed to Jesus. He dared to expand and even amend the Law, and he challenged their authority in the Temple itself (11:15f.). He was regarded as some form of Messiah. If this were so, then he was not only blasphemous but a danger to the security of the state. Unlike the Pharisees whose whole lives were centred on religion, the Sadducees were active in politics because they wanted to maintain their position of wealth and security.

Scribes

The Scribes belonged mainly, though not exclusively, to the party of the Pharisees. They were lawyers and sometimes are referred to as such in the Gospel.

The Scribes first appear in the reign of Solomon. They became important in the world where few could write. Originally they were responsible for making faithful copies of the scriptures and for guarding the text against any errors. Slowly they became the legal authorities on the religious Law, adding comments and interpretations of their own. As scholars of the Law they were represented in the Sanhedrin.

If parents wished their son to become a Scribe they took him to Jerusalem at the age of thirteen and enrolled him in one of the Rabbinical schools. His period of study lasted to the age of thirty when he became a Doctor of the Law.

Herodians

Little is known of this group. They were supporters of the Herod family and therefore, also of Rome. They were found mainly in Galilee, the territory of Herod himself. They were not a religious sect although some of them believed that Herod the Great was the Messiah.

The Temple

The Temple was central to Jewish belief. It symbolised the presence of God among the people.

The idea of the Temple went back to the time of Moses when God commanded a tabernacle (i.e. a tent) to be built in which to keep the Ark of the Covenant. The Ark was a portable shrine which accompanied the Israelites in their wanderings in the Sinai desert (Exodus 25 and 26).

The first Temple dates from the reign of King Solomon, c.970–930 BC and was built in Jerusalem. It was the centre of the Jewish religion. Only there could sacrificial worship take place (1 Kings 6).

This Temple was destroyed in 586 BC by the Babylonians. In 520 BC, on their return from exile, the Jews rebuilt the Temple.

A new and more splendid Temple was begun by Herod the Great in 20 BC. This was the Temple Jesus knew although it was not completed until after his death in 64 AD. Six years later, in 70 AD, this new Temple was destroyed by the Romans. Herod's Temple was a magnificent building. It included the following features:

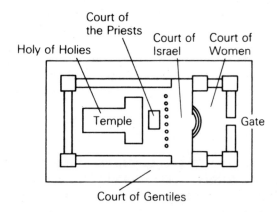

Court of Gentiles

(a) **Court of the Gentiles**. This was a public place used as a market where traders sold the birds and animals used for sacrifices.

In this court could be found the money changers who changed the 'unclean' currencies such as Roman money into the sacred Temple money for the payment of Temple collections.

(b) **Court of Israel**. Only Jewish males were allowed in this court. Gentiles were forbidden to enter. There was a separate court for women. Again, Gentiles were not allowed to enter.

(c) **Court of the Priests**. This was the most exclusive court. Only the priests were allowed to enter. In this area was the altar of sacrifice on which the birds and animals were killed.

(d) **Holy of Holies**. The Holy of Holies was the innermost shrine of the Temple. It was screened by a large veil or curtain. Behind it was the altar of incense.

The Holy of Holies was reserved for the presence of God. No one but the officiating priest was allowed to enter the Holy of Holies.

Temple Worship

The importance of the Temple worship, for the Jew of Jesus' day, can hardly be overestimated. The idea of sacrifice was central to this worship. There were three different types of sacrifice.

(a) **Morning and evening sacrifice**. Both took the form of the offering of incense; the sacrifice of a lamb without blemish;

the meal offering of flour and oil; all of which was accompanied by prayer and praise.

(b) **Private offerings – daily**. Each day individuals would ask for private sacrifices to be offered to God in thanksgiving or forgiveness for sins.

(c) **Feast days**. On Feast days such as Passover, thousands of offerings were made.

All sacrifices, bloody or bloodless, were intended as a means of obtaining the forgiveness of God. The climax of the sacrificial year was the Day of Atonement when the High Priest entered the Holy of Holies and offered the blood of sacrifice as atonement for all the sins of Israel.

Once a year, at the Feast of Passover, vast numbers of Jewish pilgrims came to Jerusalem from all over to celebrate the Exodus. At this time the Temple resembled a huge slaughterhouse as thousands of lambs were sacrificed and handed to the people for the celebration of the Passover meal that night.

Temple worship ceased after the destruction of the Temple in 70 AD. All that remains of Herod the Great's Temple is a course of huge stones where the Jews meet daily for prayer. This is known as the Western Wall (popularly called the Wailing Wall because Jews bewail the destruction of the Temple there).

The Synagogue

There was only one Temple but there was a synagogue in every Jewish community. The word 'synagogue' is a Greek word meaning 'assembly' or 'meeting' and represents the gathering of a congregation. Like the word 'church', the synagogue came to stand for the building as well as the people meeting there.

The origin of the synagogue goes back to the Babylonian period. The Jews were in exile after 586 BC and found themselves cut off from the Temple. They evolved a form of worship which required neither priest, Temple nor sacrifice. They gathered together to read the scriptures and to pray. They found this to be so worthwhile that, on their return from exile, synagogue worship continued and became a major influence in religious life.

The synagogue was administered by a council of 'elders' who appointed a 'ruler' whose duty it was to prepare for the daily services and provide some general supervision. There were three services each day, at 9.00 am; 12.00 noon and 3.00 pm.

Synagogue worship is very important to the Jews. Since the destruction of the Temple in 70 AD, it has been the synagogue that has kept the Jewish faith alive throughout the centuries even to the present day.

Understanding Mark's Gospel

In the earliest years of the Christian Church there was little need for a written record of the events of Jesus' life, death and resurrection. They had been observed by the disciples and passed on by word of mouth. That was sufficient because the early Christians expected Jesus to return immediately and set up the reign of God on earth. (This event is called the Parousia.)

As Christianity spread through the Roman Empire, so the stories of Jesus also spread. It is natural that some of these stories were developed and adapted to make the message of the Gospel relevant to people of differing cultures to the Jews.

In 66 AD the Jews rebelled against their Roman overlords in Palestine. This resulted in Jerusalem being destroyed in 70 AD. James, the leader of the Jerusalem Church was killed at this time. At about the same time, far away in Rome, Christians were being persecuted by the Emperor Nero. Thousands of Christians lost their lives. Amongst them, according to tradition, were St Peter and St Paul.

Jesus had not returned and the first generation Christians were beginning to die. Now the 'Gospel', the good news about Jesus, had to be preserved. The traditions about Jesus were collected and formed into books by the Evangelists. Of the many Gospels written, the Church, later on, chose four as being the ones that contained 'the faith'. These four were the ones named Matthew, Mark, Luke and John.

At first, the reading of a Gospel may give the impression that it is a biography of Jesus. They contain a record of his birth (in Matthew and Luke only); life, death and resurrection. It would be a mistake, however, to think that Mark and the other Evangelists set out with this purpose.

Oral Tradition

After the death and resurrection of Jesus, the stories about his life were passed on by word of mouth for some thirty years before the first Gospel was written. This is called the period of the 'oral tradition'.

The study of the oral tradition is called *form criticism*. Form criticism examines the way in which the traditions of Jesus were preserved and handed on prior to the writing of the Gospels.

The form critics claim:

- The stories about Jesus can be categorised into four main 'forms'. These can be seen clearly in the Gospel narrative.
- The four forms are:

    (a) pronouncement stories (called paradigms). These are stories that lead to an important statement by Jesus. For example, the story of Jesus having dinner at Levi's house leads to Jesus telling the Pharisees, 'I did not come to invite virtuous people but sinners' (2:17);
    (b) miracle stories: (all following a set pattern);
    (c) biographical sketches. These are stories that provide more detail about a specific person (see 6:17–29); and
    (d) parables.

- The reason for the preserving and passing on of the traditions in this way was because they were used primarily by the early Church in its teaching of the community.
- The form critics claim that some development of the stories took place in the passing down of these traditions.
- Each story was separate and passed on in isolation with the possible exception of the story of the Passion.
- The context of each story in the Gospel was at the sole discretion of the author.

When each Evangelist recorded the stories about Jesus he did so for a particular purpose. He did not write a biography. He wrote with a particular audience in mind and therefore emphasised the points of interest most suited to that audience. The study of the author's influence on the oral tradition is called *redaction criticism*.

The redaction critics claim:

- It is important to realise that the Gospel writers were not writing history as we understand it.

- They were not interested in the question 'what really happened?' They took for granted the historical events of Jesus; his birth; life; death; and resurrection. The question they sought to answer was much more important. They asked continually, 'What does this mean for us?'

  For example they would ask: 'What does it mean for Jesus to die on the Cross?' rather than 'What happened when Jesus was crucified?'
- It is inevitable that the Evangelist made changes to the traditions in his desire to say what the events of Jesus' life meant for his readers.

Who was Mark?

The New Testament mentions a John Mark quite a lot. If this is the same person as the author of the Gospel then it is possible to build up a picture of him.

(a) He lived in Jerusalem. There is a story in the Acts of the Apostles which describes how Peter, after he had escaped from prison went to the house of Mary, the mother of John Mark (Acts 12:12).

(b) His names – John, a Jewish name and Mark, a Latin name – suggest that he was a Greek-speaking Jew. They were called Hellenists.

(c) John Mark was not an apostle, yet he seems to have been closely involved with three of the principal characters of the early Church:

Peter sends greetings from Rome from himself and Mark, who he calls 'my son' (1 Peter 5:13);

Barnabas was Mark's cousin and he stood by him when there was a dispute with Paul (Acts 15:36–40);

Paul was helped by Mark during the time when he was captive in Rome (Colossians 4:10; 2 Timothy 4:11). These connections cannot be proved. Mark, after all, was one of the most common names in the Roman Empire.

(d) None of the Gospels contain the name of the author in the text. The titles were added later by the Church. It is quite likely, however, that there is a reference to the author in the young man who escaped and ran away naked (14:51) at the arrest of Jesus. This seems the only explanation of this verse that makes any sense.

(e) All the early evidence of the Church is unanimous in saying that Mark is the author of the Gospel and that he was closely connected with Peter. Bishop Eusebius (c.260–340) quotes Papias, a Bishop in Asia Minor in about 140 AD, who in turn quotes John the Elder who says: '. . . Mark, having become the interpreter of Peter, wrote down accurately, though not in order, all that he remembered of the things said and done by the Lord. . .' There is also the quotation from Irenaeus (one of the early Church Fathers 140–202 AD) who had been in Rome. Writing a hundred years before Eusebius, he states that after the deaths of Peter and Paul, in the course of the persecutions in Rome: 'Mark, the disciple and interpreter of Peter, also handed down to us in writing the things preached by Peter.'

(f) It would be a mistake, however, to think that the Markan Gospel of the New Testament is merely the notes of, or the preaching of Peter. Whatever information Mark received from Peter it is certain that, by the time he wrote his finished Gospel, development and adaptation of much of the material had taken place. Indeed, many of the stories were already in existence in an oral form.

The Characteristics of the Gospel

(1)   The Gospel was written in primitive Greek. It has been suggested that Greek was not the native language of the author but that he wrote in the universal language of the day which was Greek, while thinking in his own language which was probably Aramaic.

(2)   There are certain details in the Gospel which make scholars think that there is an authentic eye-witness standing behind the Gospel story in some of the accounts. In view of the evidence of the early Fathers of the Christian Church, this was most probably Peter. There is, for example, a mention of a 'cushion' in the calming of the storm (4:38) and of 'green grass' in the feeding of the 5000 (6:39).

(3)   The Gospel is not written for Jewish readers. Mark explains Jewish customs and Aramaic expressions throughout the book. For example, he translates the word 'Golgotha' (15:22) and 'Eli, Eli, lema sabachthani' (15:34).

(4)   The major theme of the Gospel is *suffering*. It is not surprising that this is so considering the background in Rome against which the Gospel is written. Jesus is the Messiah who must suffer and die in order to rise from the dead and return to establish God's kingdom on earth. Suffering is so prominent a part of the Gospel that it has

been described as a Passion story with an introduction. The rumblings of death appear as early as 3:6 after the stories of conflict with the religious authorities. From chapter 8 onwards the theme of suffering is the major preoccupation of the book. The final week of Jesus occupies one-third of the Gospel.

The Date of the Gospel

If the Gospel was written by the John Mark who is mentioned in the Acts of the Apostles, then it must have been written in the first generation of the Christian Church, between 35 and 75 AD.

Peter was probably martyred in Rome during the persecutions of Nero in 64–65 AD. An early prologue attached to Mark's Gospel says that Mark wrote after the death of Peter in Italy. Irenaeus says that Mark wrote after the deaths of Peter and Paul, while Clement of Alexandria states that the book was written while Peter was still preaching in Rome. Therefore, the date of the Gospel is likely to have been in the decade 60–70 AD.

The Gospel contains a large amount of material concerned with the theme of suffering and persecution. It is reasonable to assume, therefore, that it was written during or immediately after the persecutions in Rome. This would date the book around 65–70 AD.

Most of the early Christian authorities claim the place of writing was Rome although St Jerome, writing much later, says the Gospel was written in Alexandria. This seems unlikely in view of the overwhelming claim of the early authorities that the Gospel was written in Rome.

2 The Identity of Jesus

The purpose of this chapter is to discover the identity of Jesus as found in Mark's Gospel. This identity can be discovered by examining the following.

- The major titles used of Jesus in the Gospel.
- The title used by Jesus himself in the Gospel.
- Other titles used by the disciples, opponents and Mark himself.

The Major Titles Used of Jesus in the Gospel

In the very first verse of the Gospel we find a statement of Mark's own view of Jesus.

> Here begins the Gospel of Jesus Christ the Son of God (1:1).

In this 'title' verse of the Gospel Mark uses three very different names for Jesus: Jesus, Christ, and Son of God.

Jesus (the man)

> Here begins the Gospel of JESUS Christ the Son of God (1:1).

The first 'title' is the personal name 'Jesus'. This was a fairly common Jewish name which means 'God is Salvation'. Mark uses it as a name to show the humanity of Jesus as he tells the story of Jesus in his Gospel. He uses the name regularly. It occurs eighty-one times in the Gospel, but there are only three occasions when characters in the Gospel narrative call Jesus by his personal name. Twice it is by demoniacs (these are people who are possessed by an unclean spirit) (1:24; 5:7); and once it is by the blind beggar called Bartimaeus who wishes to be healed (10:47).

The most typical way in which Mark identifies Jesus is by using the phrase 'Jesus of Nazareth'. Nazareth is a town in Galilee (1:9,24; 10:47; 14:67; 16:6).

Mark tells us a lot about Jesus the man. He was a carpenter by trade (6:3). According to tradition, Jesus left his trade when he was in his late twenties and began to travel around Galilee as:

– a preacher (1:38–39);
– a teacher (1:21; 10:1); and
– a healer and exorcist (someone who can cast out evil
  spirits) (1:32–34; 3:10–11; 6:55–56).

He attracted large crowds and wandered about the
synagogues, villages and region of Galilee (1:33, 38–39, 45;
2:13; 3:7–8; 4:1); travelling across the Sea of Galilee to Gentile
country and back (4:35; 5:1; 6:45; 8:10).

Sometimes he would seek the peace of the lonely place so
he could be either by himself or just with his disciples (1:35,
45; 6:31–32). On other occasions he would go off into the
hills (3:13; 6:46; 9:2).

He was misunderstood by his own family (3:21) and
gathered together a new 'family' from those who followed
him (3:31–35; 10:29–30).

He became hated by the Jewish leaders because he made
comments about Jewish customs and traditions (2:18f.;
2:27–3:6) and also because he mixed with tax-collectors and
sinners (2:15–17), Gentiles (3:8; 5:1–20) and outcasts (1:40–45).

It is this same man Jesus who in all his travels and
dealings with people showed many human emotions. It is
important to remember that, of all the human characteristics
that Mark gives to Jesus, the one he both begins and ends
with is the simple human title of a *man* who comes from
Nazareth (1:9; 16:6). Mark presents Jesus as a human being
and he uses the name Jesus to do just that; to show that this
man is the same as us with many of the same emotions and
characteristics.

Jesus: the man for today

What meaning does Mark's picture of Jesus as a man have for people today?

*Many people today seem to have forgotten that Jesus was a
human being. They make comments such as 'Jesus knew
everything that was going to happen' or 'Jesus could perform
miracles, because he was God'. Such comments give the
impression that Jesus was God pretending to be a man or that he
was some super-human figure. This is not what the Church
teaches.*

*There are two reasons why it is important to realise that Jesus
was a man.*

As a man, Jesus experienced the things human beings experience; emotions such as love, anger, anxiety, sorrow and distress. It is because he understood these emotions that Christians believe Jesus understands them. The story of Jesus in the Garden of Gethsemane, for example, shows the human emotions of anxiety and distress experienced by Jesus; human emotions felt by most people at some time in their lives (14:32–42).

More importantly, Jesus is presented as a man who shows what it means to live a human life according to God's will. In his life Jesus came across temptation, opposition, hatred, suffering and even death, all because he refused to turn his back on what he understood to be God's will.

> Abba Father. . .all things are possible to thee; take this cup away from me. Yet not what I will but what thou wilt (14:36).

Christians believe Jesus is the perfect example of obedience to God and that he invites other people to follow that obedience in their own lives. He says to his disciples,

> Anyone who wishes to be a follower of mine must leave self behind; he must take up his cross, and come with me (8:34).

In other words Christians are encouraged to follow the example of Jesus because he showed them how a human being could live a life perfectly dedicated to God.

The Christ

> Here begins the Gospel of Jesus CHRIST the Son of God (1:1).

The word 'Christ' means 'anointed one'. 'Christ' is a Greek word. In Hebrew the same word is 'Messiah'. It is important to realise that the words 'Christ' and 'Messiah' are the same word.

– *Christ* (Greek);
– *Messiah* (Hebrew);
– *Anointed one* (English).

It is also important to realise that the word 'Christ' is a title given to Jesus. It is not a surname. To be accurate we should never say 'Jesus Christ' but 'Jesus *the* Christ'. The background to the title 'Christ' is Jewish. In Israel, High Priests and Kings were anointed with oil as a sign that they had been chosen and appointed by God.

The Jews believed their God was all-powerful and controlled the destiny of all nations. This belief received a severe test after Israel had been defeated by Babylon in the sixth century BC. The Jews had been taken from their own country and made captives in Babylon. During this period the Jews began to hope for a leader who would unite the nation and make it great once again. They remembered the days of King David. They remembered the promise of Moses. . . 'The Lord your God will raise up a prophet from among you like myself, and you shall listen to him' (Deuteronomy 18:15).

Slowly the idea of the 'Messiah' figure developed; a Messiah who would come in the future. He would be the descendant of David; chosen by God and who would rule as King. His reign would bring peace. God's rule would be established on earth.

There was no set view of how God would bring the Messiah to the world. The main beliefs can be summarised:

1   the Messiah would be the representative of God who would stand against the enemies of God and of his chosen people;
2   all faithful Jews, including those who lived outside Palestine would be gathered into Palestine;
3   Jerusalem and the Holy Temple would become the centre of the world; and
4   the Messiah would bring about a period of perfect happiness and peace and God's rule of justice and mercy would be established for ever.

Unfortunately by the time of Jesus the great hope of the Messiah had been watered down into the popular figure of an earthly warrior who would come to free Israel from the occupation of the Romans.

The title 'Christ' or 'Messiah' is a very rare one in Mark's Gospel. At first it may seem surprising that the title 'Christ' does not appear more often in the Gospel. However, the explanation may be simple. Jesus did not speak of himself as Christ because he did not wish to be thought of as the popular military leader who would free Israel from the

Romans. So when, at Caesarea Philippi, Peter makes his profession of faith. . .

> You are the Messiah *(8:27–30)*;

Jesus warns his disciples not to tell anyone. Only at the end, during the trial before the Sanhedrin, does Jesus admit his Messiahship. The High Priest asks

> 'Are you the Messiah, the Son of the Blessed One?'
> Jesus said, 'I am. . .' *(14:61)*.

At this point in the Gospel there is nothing to be served by not using the title. Jesus knows the end is near and that there can be no turning back. Even though the actual title is rare Jesus did act as Messiah. For example, he rode into Jerusalem on Palm Sunday as a Messianic King.

> Hosanna! Blessings on him who comes in the name
> of the Lord!. . . *(11:9; cf. Psalm 118: 25–26)*.

In addition, there can be no doubt that in the work and words of Jesus the Church came quickly to the certainty in faith that Jesus was the long awaited Messiah of God.

Son of God

> Here begins the Gospel of Jesus Christ THE SON
> OF GOD *(1:1)*.

This is the most popular title given to Jesus today and it has the full weight of 2000 years' thought behind it.

Perhaps the title is too easily used today. In Mark's Gospel it is, like 'Christ', a rare title.

As with the title 'Christ' the origin goes back to the Old Testament, where the nation Israel, which thought of God as a father, is often referred to as the 'son of God'. One of the most famous verses is found in the prophet Hosea, where God says, 'When Israel was a boy, I loved him;/I called my son out of Egypt' (Hosea 11:1). By the time of Jesus the 'Son of God' was regarded as being a Messianic title referring to the one who was to come to do all that the Messiah would do. It is the title that expresses the closest possible relationship between Jesus and God.

There are five major texts in the Gospel which deal with this title 'Son of God'.

1   Here begins the Gospel of Jesus Christ the Son of God *(1:1)*.

Mark starts his Gospel in a way which reminds us of the book of Genesis, the first book of the Old Testament. In Genesis it is the beginning of creation. In Mark it is the beginning of the 'Good News' (this is what the word Gospel means) which begins with the coming of God's Son. This is Mark's own statement of faith. The Son of God is a divine person. He is from God.

So Mark opens his Gospel with this statement of divine sonship. He begins his Gospel with the title 'Son of God' and repeats the title at the moment of death: 'Truly this man was a son of God' (15:39).

2   Truly this man was a son of God *(15:39)*.

This is the climax of the Gospel. At the moment of death on the cross the Roman centurion, who had watched the event of the crucifixion, makes this same confession with which the Gospel began. Jesus is the Son of God. In between these beginning and concluding statements of faith in Jesus, the title is used three times.

3   Thou art my Son, my Beloved; on thee my favour rests *(1:11)*.

At the moment of Jesus' baptism, Mark describes how the voice of God speaks words which show the close relationship between God and Jesus. He is the 'Beloved Son'. Jesus, as the anointed one (Messiah), is chosen and appointed by his Father for all His work.

4   This is my Son, my Beloved; listen to him *(9:7)*.

When Jesus, accompanied by Peter, James and John was up the mountain the voice of God spoke again of the close relationship between himself and Jesus. This is the crowning glory of Jesus in Mark's Gospel. He is God's 'Beloved Son' and as such his disciples are commanded to listen to him.

5   He had now only one left to send, his own dear (beloved) son. In the end he sent him *(12:6)*.

In the parable of the *Wicked Husbandmen* or *The Tenants in the Vineyard*, which deals with the theme of the history of man's salvation, the beloved son is sent by the owner of the vineyard (God), after all attempts to communicate with the tenants (Jewish leaders) through the servants (prophets) had failed. This was to fail too for the tenants 'seized him and killed him and flung his body out of the vineyard'.

It is very important to note that the word 'beloved' is used on all three occasions. This indicates the closest possible relationship between Jesus and his Father.

In summary, the meaning of the title 'Son of God' in Mark's Gospel is that Jesus is a special person; a person in the tradition of the Old Testament; a person chosen and given a mission by God. Mark makes this person especially important by showing the personal relationship in which Jesus stands as the 'Beloved' – a Son, special beyond words.

Here begins the Gospel of Jesus Christ the Son of God	Thou art My Son; My Beloved; on thee my favour rests	This is My Son; My Beloved Listen to Him	He had now only one left to send, his own beloved son	This man was a son of God
1 : 1	**1 : 11**	**9 : 7**	**12 : 6**	**15 : 39**
Showing faith in Jesus by Mark	Confirming faith in Jesus by God	Command to Jesus' followers to take notice of him	Forecast of the death of Jesus	Showing faith in Jesus repeated

Jesus: the Christ, the Son of God for today

What meaning does Mark's picture of Jesus as the Christ, the Son of God have for people today?
Many people have difficulty in understanding what God is really like. This is not surprising. God is not a human being. Even when God is called 'Father' it is only an image that is being used. Unlike a human father God is everywhere; he is all-powerful; he is perfect. Such ideas have always been hard for people to understand.

Christians believe Jesus provides the answer to the question, 'What is God really like?'. When they look at

*Jesus, he is like a window through which they can see God.
Jesus is someone ordinary that human beings can understand,
yet he is believed to mirror the perfect qualities of God.*

*For example, God's love for people is shown in the way
Jesus cared for those who were sick or outcast in society
such as the tax-collector (2:15–17). God's desire for all people
to come to him is shown in the way Jesus was willing to die
to convince them of his love. Christians believe Jesus does
this because he is the 'Son of God'.*

*We should remember that Mark makes it clear, with the
possible exception of the reply to the High Priest's question
at the trial before the Sanhedrin, that Jesus never claimed to
be either Christ or Son of God. Nevertheless, it is also true
that the Christian Church from the beginning used both these
titles when talking about Jesus.*

*What the early Christians meant by calling Jesus both
Christ and Son of God was that they saw God at work in
him; in his life, death and resurrection. So they could say, as
did the centurion,*

Truly this man was a son of God (15:39).

*The same declaration of faith is made by present day
Christians.*

*We have already seen how the Jews believed in a
representative of God called the Christ, who would come in the
future, bringing peace and setting up God's rule on earth.
Christians today see in Jesus that same Christ figure who has
come and who has and will establish God's rule on earth. It must
be remembered that the daily prayer of the Christian includes the
words, 'Your kingdom come, Your will be done, on earth as it is
in heaven'.*

*Just as the Jews came to hope for a Messiah who would free
them from all their sufferings, so Christians have always thought
of Jesus the Christ as one who came to guide them through such
times and bring them back to God.*

*In our own day the world is not, at times, a happy place.
Evils and injustices such as violence, poverty and starvation still
bring suffering to many. The Christian disciple is committed to
fighting all injustice. Outstanding examples of such discipleship
can be found throughout history. Two such examples are Dr
Albert Schweitzer who struggled against leprosy in the damp
disease-ridden forests of Africa; or the Rev. Dr Martin Luther*

King *who strived for equal human rights for all in the United
States of America.*

*Today we find Mother Teresa of Calcutta working in the slums
of India amongst extreme poverty. Other numerous Christian
organisations continue to work in many areas of the world in the
fight against starvation to bring in God's reign of justice and
love.*

*It must be remembered that many non-Christian individuals and
organisations also work against these injustices because of their
own beliefs about the world and our place in it.*

*The Christian is commanded as a follower of the Christ to
stand against the evils in the world; to speak out against all
injustice and to work for the peace and harmony of all people
under God.*

Study Skills

Knowledge

1 Write out the first verse of Mark's Gospel.
2 What does the word Jesus mean?
3 Name four human qualities of Jesus and give an example of
   each from Mark's Gospel.
4 What do the words Christ/Messiah mean?
5 What did the Jews expect the Messiah to do?
6 In which two stories does God call Jesus his son?
7 On which occasion did Jesus admit he was the Christ?
8 What did the centurion say just after the death of Jesus?
9 What word is used by Mark to show the close relationship
   between God and Jesus?
10 In which three passages does this word appear?

Understanding

11 At the time of Jesus some Jews held a popular idea of the role
    of the Messiah. What was this idea? How did Jesus show he
    was different from their expectation?
12 'Jesus was a real human being.' How far does Mark show Jesus
    to be a man? Illustrate your answer with examples from Mark's
    Gospel.
13 Using the metaphor of a window, explain how Christians can
    think of Jesus as both human and divine.

Evaluation

14 In what ways do you think it is helpful for Christians to
    remember Jesus was a real human being like themselves?

15 What does it mean for Christians today to believe that Jesus was 'the Christ, the Son of God'?

Practical Work

- Look up the following stories. In each one there can be found a human emotion shown by Jesus. In each case say briefly what the story is about and then state the emotion Jesus shows. (1:40–45; 3:1–6; 6:1–6; 10:13–16; 10:17–22; 14:32–42; 15:33–39).
- Choose one of the following Christians; Dr Albert Schweitzer; the Rev. Dr Martin Luther King or Mother Teresa of Calcutta. Find out how they have tried to follow Jesus in their life and work.

The Title Used by Jesus in the Gospel

Son of Man

This is the main title in Mark's Gospel which Jesus uses of himself. Perhaps Jesus called himself by this mysterious uncommon name so that he could carry on his mission safely without making an open claim to Messiahship. Such a claim would either be misunderstood or bring about a speedy end to his ministry. Once again the title has its roots in the Old Testament, where in Hebrew poetry it meant simply 'a man' or 'man' in general. For example: 'What is man that thou shouldst remember him,/mortal man (lit. Son of Man) that thou shouldst care for him?' (Psalm 8:4).

However in the Old Testament book of Daniel, the phrase takes on a special meaning. In chapter 7 there is an account of one of Daniel's dreams or visions. He sees four great beasts appear from the sea, savage and terrifying. Then he sees an old man sitting as though in judgement and 'one like a son of man' (Daniel 7:13) is presented to him on 'the clouds of heaven'. He is brought before the old man, honoured by him and given power and glory.

The interpretation of the dream is also given. The beasts stand for the nations such as Babylon who had oppressed the Jews, and the human figure of the Son of Man represents 'the Saints of the Most High'. These are God's loyal few who were ready to go to their deaths rather than deny their faith in God. They will be given their place in heaven.

Is this the way in which Jesus uses the title? Surprisingly, there are only three occasions when the term 'Son of Man' is used in the Gospel connected with the ideas contained in Daniel (where they carry the idea of Jesus being cast in the role of one who will come in power and glory on 'the clouds of heaven' at the end of time; this second coming is called the Parousia). All three of them have to do with the subject of persecution of either Jesus or his followers.

The first is from a passage on what it means to be a disciple.

> If anyone is ashamed of me and mine in this wicked and godless age, the Son of Man will be ashamed of him, when he comes in the glory of his Father and of the holy angels (8:38).

The second verse comes from the trial of Jesus before the Jewish council (called the Sanhedrin) where Jesus is asked by the High Priest if he is the Christ. Jesus replies that he is, and goes on to say:

> . . .and you will see the Son of Man seated at the right hand of God and coming with the clouds of heaven (14:62).

The third verse comes from the Apocalytpic Chapter (See chapter 10). In this Jesus is talking about the signs of the end of the world.

> Then they will see the Son of Man coming in the clouds with great power and glory. . . (13:26).

There is a close similarity between what is said about the Son of Man in Mark and the picture of the righteous few in Daniel. This is a picture of men and women suffering because of their faith in, and loyalty to, God. They will win through in the end.

In the first of these passages the disciples are challenged to remain faithful in spite of persecution. They must take up the cross and follow Jesus (8:34). In the second passage we find the comment that so angered the Sanhedrin that they passed the death sentence on Jesus. In the third passage Jesus comments on the end of the world and the return of the Son of Man.

Two more Son of Man sayings in Mark's Gospel concern the question of authority. Christians believe this authority is given to Jesus by God, for Jesus claims to do things that only God can do. In this sense he is acting as the divine representative in the Daniel sense.

...the Son of Man has the right on earth to forgive sins *(2:10)*.

...the Son of Man is sovereign even over the Sabbath *(2:28)*.

(This means that the authority of Jesus is greater than the Sabbath law.)

All the other sayings about the Son of Man in Mark deal with the themes of suffering, death and resurrection. This is only a small part of the theme in the book of Daniel. There are eight such sayings in Mark:

1 And he began to teach them that the Son of Man had to undergo great sufferings, and to be rejected by the elders, chief priests, and doctors of the law; to be put to death, and to rise again three days afterwards *(8:31)*.

2 After the Transfiguration, Jesus warned the disciples

   not to tell anyone what they had seen until the Son of Man had risen from the dead *(9:9)*.

3 ...the Son of Man...is to endure great sufferings and to be treated with contempt *(9:12)*.

4 The Son of Man is now to be given up into the power of men, and they will kill him, and three days after being killed, he will rise again *(9:31)*.

5 We are going up to Jerusalem...and the Son of Man will be given up to the chief priests and the doctors of the law; they will condemn him to death and hand him over to the foreign power. He will be mocked and spat upon, flogged and killed; and three days afterwards, he will rise again *(10:33–34)*.

6 For even the Son of Man did not come to be served but to serve, and to give up his life as a ransom for many *(10:45)*.

7 At the Last Supper Jesus tells his disciples:

   The Son of Man is going the way appointed for him in the scriptures *(14:21)*.

8 In the Garden of Gethsemane Jesus says to his disciples:

> The hour has come. The Son of Man is betrayed to sinful men. Up, let us go forward! My betrayer is upon us (14:41–42).

The main theme in these passages is suffering; far more than is to be found in the ideas of Daniel. We must look elsewhere for an answer to the question of what Jesus meant by the use of the title Son of Man.

There is another Old Testament book where we might find the answer. In Isaiah there is a collection of songs (poems) about someone called 'the Servant of the Lord'. These are sometimes called the 'Suffering Servant Songs' and the person in them is called 'the Suffering Servant'. It would seem that Jesus combined the idea of the Son of Man from Daniel with the Suffering Servant of Isaiah. For example, in Isaiah 53 we find: 'He was despised. . . tormented and humbled by suffering; we despised him. . .Yet on himself he bore our sufferings. . .' (Isaiah 53:3–4). His suffering was not of his own making but was a punishment for the sins of others. This was the role of both the suffering Servant and Jesus:

> For even the Son of Man did not come to be served but to serve, and to give up his life as a ransom for many (10:45).

This joining of the functions of the Son of Man and the Suffering Servant is unique to the Gospels. It has no parallel in Jewish literature.

SUMMARY

The term 'Son of Man' is used in two main ways in Mark's Gospel:

1 Jesus suffers as the Son of Man to save people from their sins (the theme of Isaiah).
2 Jesus will return as Son of Man; as judge, in power and glory, to set up the rule of God on earth (the theme of Daniel).

It must be remembered that this is the title Jesus uses of himself. Nowhere is Jesus called Son of Man by anyone else.

Jesus: the Son of Man for today

What meaning does Mark's picture of Jesus as the Son of Man have for people today?

This is the most difficult title for twentieth century Christians as they rarely use the title in everyday thinking and speaking about Jesus. However, the title is of great importance.

The title 'Son of Man' still tells of a time when Jesus will return and assist in judgement. There is a tendency today to think that everyone will finally be with God in heaven; that His love is so great that He will not turn away anyone however wicked that person is. Others feel it would be a mistake to allow the pendulum to swing too far the other way and think of God as someone who takes delight in condemning people, but insist that the New Testament speaks of judgement as well as God's mercy. It warns that there will be a time when humanity will be faced with judgement. Mark states that the disciple who is 'ashamed' of Jesus will face the same treatment at the time of judgement (8:38). A person's discipleship will be judged.

Such an idea of judgement makes sense when it is placed in the context of the suffering of the Son of Man in Mark's Gospel. This idea of suffering is central to the Gospel and is important in any age.

Christianity has always been based on the belief that Jesus came to save people from the power of sin. He came to call people back to God. His opening words in Mark's Gospel are a summary of his whole message;

> The time has come: the Kingdom of God is upon
> you; repent, and believe the Gospel (1:15).

This message he gave by teaching and healing. The message was ignored, instead Jesus was rejected and executed. By his death, however, Jesus showed his love for both God and humanity. He was willing to die to show people how much God wished them to belong to him.

This sacrifice of Jesus, made willingly, was not to end in death but in resurrection. As Mark says,

> The Son of Man is now to be given up into the
> power of men, and they will kill him, and three
> days after being killed, he will rise again (9:31).

So Christians believe that a person who responds to this and accepts the death and resurrection of Jesus as the way in which they can be united with God, will be saved from the power of evil which is called sin. This is what it means to call Jesus, 'Son of Man'.

Other Titles Used by the Disciples, Opponents and Mark Himself

Throughout the Gospel various other titles can be found that play only a minor role in our search for the identity of Jesus. For example, Jesus applies the title 'prophet' to himself when quoting a well known saying,

> A prophet will always be held in honour except in his own home town, and among his kinsmen and family (6:4).

A prophet in the Old Testament was someone who called the people back to God, warning them of the consequences if they did not obey. Christians believed that Jesus was more than just a prophet. The idea of believing in Jesus as a prophet seems to have been a false view some people had of Jesus (6:16; 8:28).

Teacher (Rabbi) (Master)
Mark uses this term frequently. It is used (fourteen times) by the disciples (4:38; 9:5; 9:38; 10:35); strangers (5:35; 9:17; 10:17–20, 51); and opponents (12:14; 12:19; 14:45). Once Jesus uses it of himself (14:14). Teaching is an important part of Jesus' mission in the Gospel but Mark makes it clear that the reputation of Jesus is not in him being a teacher. His teaching is based on the fact that he is the Son of God (1:1; 1:22; 11:27–33). So 'teacher', 'rabbi' or 'master' serve as terms of human respect.

Beelzebul (3:22–30)
This is a rare local name for the prince of devils, Satan. The accusation against Jesus is that his power to cast out evil spirits comes from Beelzebul, the prince of devils himself. Jesus answers this by showing how illogical the argument is. Surely Satan would not cast himself out? (See chapter 6.)

Lord
The title 'Lord' is not used in Mark in the sense of calling Jesus 'the Lord'. This title was only given to Jesus after the resurrection and indicates his divine authority over all things.

In Mark's Gospel the word is used simply to mean 'sir' or 'master' (7:28).

Variants on the Messianic Title

(a) **King of the Jews** (15:2, 9, 12, 18, 26, 32). This is only used in the trial of Jesus before Pontius Pilate and at the Crucifixion. It is used in disbelief by Pilate and in jest by the Jewish leaders but Mark is using it as a Messianic title (see chapter 8).

(b) **Son of David** (10:47, 48). This is the title used by the blind man called Bartimaeus who tries to attract the attention of Jesus because he wants him to cure his blindness. Once again, it is meant to be understood that Jesus is the Messiah as the Jews believed that the Messiah would be a descendant of King David (see chapter 4).

(c) **Holy One of God** (1:24). This is the title used by the man with the unclean spirit in the synagogue at Capernaum. The evil spirit is quite capable of recognising the divinity of Jesus and is frightened by his power.

> What do you want with us Jesus of Nazareth? Have you come to destroy us? I know who you are – the Holy One of God *(1:24)*.

This is very near to calling Jesus the Son of God (see chapter 4).

(d) **Son of the Most High God** (5:7). Once again it is a demoniac who has the insight into the person of Jesus.

> What do you want with me, Jesus, son of the Most High God? In God's name do not torment me *(5:7)*.

In fear he calls Jesus by this name which is the same as calling him the Son of God. (See chapter 4.)

SUMMARY

What then can we say about the identity of Jesus in Mark's Gospel?

1 It is important to state at the outset that Jesus is a human figure. *Jesus is a man.*
2 All the other titles with one exception point to him

being also *the Christ* who is *Son of God*. He is the Christ who is *King of Israel* (15:32); Christ **the Son of the Blessed One** (14:61); Christ **the Son of David** (12:35) and above all **Jesus Christ the Son of God** (1:1).

3   In sharp contrast to these Messianic titles there is also the name Jesus seemed to prefer: *the Son of Man*. This title is always separated from that of the Messiah. The Gospel never says that the Christ is the Son of Man.

The Son of Man is one who must suffer and die but who will be raised from the dead. He will be given power and will return in glory to assist in the judgement of God and the setting up of God's Kingdom on earth.

Study Skills

Knowledge

1   According to Mark, which title did Jesus use to refer to himself?
2   What is the origin of the phrase 'Son of Man'?
3   Which Old Testament book talks about the 'Son of Man'?
4   Which Old Testament prophet writes about the Suffering Servant?
5   Give an account of the theme of suffering contained in the sayings of the 'Son of Man' in Mark's Gospel.
6   Name three Messianic titles in Mark's Gospel other than Messiah/Christ or Son of God.

Understanding

7   Explain the importance of the title 'Son of Man' for Jesus. How does Jesus combine this title with the prophecies about the Suffering Servant?
8   Explain carefully how Mark uses the title 'King of the Jews'. What do you think Mark means by this title?

Evaluation

9   In what ways do you think the title 'Son of Man' is important for Christians today?

Examination Practice

Read the passage on the following page.

'And you', he asked, 'who do you say I am'? Peter replied: 'You are the Messiah.' Then he gave them strict orders not to tell anyone about him; and he began to teach them that the Son of Man had to undergo great sufferings, and to be rejected by the elders, chief priests, and doctors of the law; to be put to death, and to rise again three days afterwards (8:29–31).

    (a) What does the Hebrew word 'Messiah' mean in English? (1)
    (b) Comment on the meaning of the title 'Son of Man'.   (4)
    (c) For what reasons may Jesus have chosen to avoid using the title 'Christ' for himself? (2)
    (d) What do you think is the importance of this story, both for Mark and for Christians today? (3)

Practical Work

- Arrange for one or two representatives of religious leaders such as a Roman Catholic priest, an Anglican priest or a non-conformist minister to give a series of short talks and answer questions on the subject of 'Who is Jesus?'

3 The Parables of the Kingdom of God

The purpose of this chapter is to look at the parables of the kingdom of God in Mark's Gospel. The following topics are examined.

- The kingdom of God.
- What is a parable?
- What is an allegory?
- Why did Jesus use parables?
- Mark's answer to why Jesus used parables.
- The meaning of the kingdom of God for today.
- The parables and their meaning for today.

   1 The Parables of the Patches and Wineskins (2:21–22).
   2 The Parable of the Sower (4:1–9, 13–20).
   3 The Parable of the Lamp (4:21–25).
   4 The Parable of the Seed Growing Secretly (4:26–29).
   5 The Parable of the Mustard Seed (4:30–32).
   6 The Parable of the Wicked Husbandmen (or The Tenants) (12:1–12).

The Kingdom of God

The Jews used this phrase to refer to the power and authority of God. They never used it to mean an earthly kingdom in the sense of an area of land which was ruled by God. It was more a question of belonging to God's kingdom by responding to him in faith and accepting his 'rule' over one's life.

The Jews looked at the kingdom of God in two different ways.

1 The kingdom of God was *present* in the sense that God guided his people at all times.
2 The kingdom of God will come in the *future* in the sense that God will be accepted by the whole world and his rule established on earth.

In the Old Testament God is often regarded as the King of Israel, and Israel as his people. Even the great kings of Israel such as Saul, David and Solomon saw themselves only as regents of God. For example the Psalms say: 'The Lord is King'/he is clothed in majesty;/The Lord clothes himself with might. . .' (Psalm 93:1), and again, 'he is holy, he is mighty,/a king who loves justice' (Psalm 99:4).

The Jews believed that God controlled everything; the forces of nature; Israel as his chosen people and also the destiny of all other nations. They looked forward to that future time when God's rule would be all over the earth. Some of them believed that it would be brought about by an ideal representative of God, an anointed one, as of old, a Messiah (see chapter 2).

Jesus says such a moment has arrived. The very first words of Jesus in Mark's Gospel are an admirable summary of this theme.

> The time has come; the kingdom of God is upon
> you; repent, and believe the Gospel (1:15).

In other words Jesus called for people to change the direction of their lives, for this is what the word repent means. They were to have faith in the Good News (this is what the word Gospel means), which was that the kingdom of God had arrived.

Jesus also announced how to enter the kingdom of God. Some people brought children to Jesus for him to touch them. The disciples tried to stop them. Jesus was angry with them.

> Let the children come to me. . .for the kingdom of
> God belongs to such as these. I tell you, whoever
> does not accept the kingdom of God like a child will
> never enter it (10:13–16).

In other words, the way to enter the kingdom of God is to become like a child, not in the sense of being childish or even innocent or pure but in the sense that a child relies on adults for life. So a person who would enter the kingdom of God depends on God in the same way.

Jesus saw the kingdom of God as something both present and future; present in himself and in the future when God's rule would be established on earth.

What is a Parable?

A parable is a simple story with a single, simple meaning. It has one central point of teaching and the details of the story make that point both clear and vivid. The meaning is not explained but is left for the listeners to work out for themselves. A true parable relates to real life. It has a Palestinian origin. The events and characters are drawn from everyday life. Parables are the method of teaching Jesus used.

What is an Allegory?

In contrast, an allegory is a story where the message is hidden in a type of code; where the characters and/or events really represent other characters and events; a story where every detail has a meaning. An allegory may depart from everyday life into a make-believe world. The story has to be decoded in order to understand its meaning.

Some scholars believe that the allegories or allegorical interpretation of the parables were the creation of either the early Christians, or of Mark himself, reflecting the belief of his church.

EXAMPLES

Read:

1   the Parable of the Mustard Seed (4:30–32);
2   the Parable of the Wicked Husbandmen (12:1–12)

Which story is a parable? Which story is an allegory?

NOTE CAREFULLY

- The parables are not just illustrations.
- They are meant to challenge and provoke.
- Some scholars believe Jesus *only* used the parable method of teaching, not allegory.
- They claim that the allegories in the Gospel are the development of parables by either the early Church or the author to drive home a point of teaching.
- The theme of *all* the parables is the central theme of the Gospel; the meaning of the kingdom of God. The

> Jews believed that God would come to reign on
> earth. They called this the Messianic Age. Jesus
> claims that this has taken place. The kingdom of God
> has arrived.

Why did Jesus use Parables?

1   Parables are simple stories, easy both to listen to and
    understand.
2   The Jews were used to listening to parables as this
    method of teaching was well established in their culture.
3   At a time when most learning was by word of mouth, the
    short story was easily remembered.
4   The hearers have to interpret the parables for themselves.
    This gave them a deeper meaning and importance. The
    interpretation became part of a person's experience.

Mark's Answer to why Jesus used Parables

There is an answer given, in Mark's Gospel, to the question,
why did Jesus teach by using parables? The answer is a very
hard one to understand.

The disciples ask Jesus what the parables mean and he
replies:

> To you the secret of the kingdom of God has been
> given; but to those who are outside everything
> comes by way of parables, so that (as Scripture says)
> they may look and look, but see nothing; they may
> hear and hear, but understand nothing; otherwise
> they might turn to God and be forgiven (4:11–12).

This is a problem. The verses seem to be saying that the
disciples understand because they have been given the secret
of the mysteries of the kingdom but those people outside the
close circle of the disciples are taught in parables so that it
will confuse them and prevent them coming into the
kingdom.

The reason Jesus used parables cannot be to hide the truth
from people. This is not the intention of teaching and it
seems out of character with what we learn about Jesus

elsewhere in the Gospel. There must be another answer to this problem.

1 The verses, taken by Mark from Isaiah 6:9–10, are meant to explain the fact that the disciples responded to Jesus, but there were many who refused to repent and stand outside because they did not recognise who Jesus was.

2 The word 'otherwise' in the text, in its original form in Hebrew carries the alternative meaning 'unless'. This removes the difficulty immediately. The translation of Mark 4:11–12 based on Isaiah 6:9–10, could be translated: 'God has given to you the secret of His Kingdom but to those outside, everything is puzzling: as it is written (in Isaiah) "they see but do not perceive, and hear but do not understand, **unless** they turn around (repent) and God forgives them."'

3 The early Christians believed that it was God's plan for the Jews to reject Jesus so that his death and resurrection could unite all people with God.

4 The verses were added to explain why the early Church's teaching was rejected by the Jews.

It would seem that the most likely explanation is that Mark believed that the purpose of the parables was to hide the truth from those whose hearts were already set against Christianity. In so doing, he has given a false picture of Jesus' own intention in the use of parable.

The meaning of the kingdom of God for today

The idea of the kingdom of God is still relevant to Christians even though the term is not widely used today. They still believe that the kingdom of God is something present in the lives of men and women.

Some say that to belong to the kingdom of God is the same as belonging to the Church. Others claim that to belong to the kingdom of God is not exactly the same as being a member of the Church. Being a member of the kingdom goes beyond simply belonging to any individual church. They believe the kingdom of God is to do with the whole person. It begins with a response to the first words of Jesus in the Gospel.

> The time has come; the kingdom of God is upon you; repent, and believe the Gospel (*1:15*).

As already stated at the beginning of the chapter, the word 'repent' means to turn around; to undergo a change of character; to turn one's back on the past and live a life directed and governed by God. It is the dedication of the whole of life to God.

Christians claim that the kingdom of God is made up of people who have repented; who have turned their backs on the negative and destructive forces of fear, selfishness and greed and have turned to those qualities of life that draw them closer to God and to each other.

When the lawyer asked Jesus which was the greatest Commandment of all, Jesus replied,

> . . .love the Lord your God with all your heart, with all your soul, with all your mind, and with all your strength. . .Love your neighbour as yourself (12:30).

The main quality of the kingdom of God is found in this idea of love of God and each other.

The parables of the kingdom, therefore, are still seen as relevant to today by all Christians. They may be set in the everyday life of 2000 years ago and therefore seem somewhat remote from modern time, but the meaning of them is still true.

The Parables and their Meaning for Today

The Parable of the Patches and the Parable of the Wineskins (2:21–22)

This is what is known as a 'double parable' or 'doublet'. That is where there are two parables side by side with identical meanings.

Jesus points out how foolish it is to sew a patch of unshrunken material onto an old garment or to put new wine, still fermenting, into old skins that have lost their pliability and have become brittle.

Meaning
A garment was a common symbol for the world. The Jewish religion was worn out and could no longer be patched. Wine was a common symbol for salvation. Jesus had not come to reform Judaism but to present something new and revolutionary. In simple terms, the old Judaism and the new Christianity do not mix. The new wine of Christianity could not be pressed into the older wineskins of Jewish practices.

This is a picturesque way of saying that there is something new and different in the ministry of Jesus that goes beyond the boundaries of Judaism. What is new is best summed up by the phrase, 'The kingdom of God is here!'.

The meaning of the parable for today

Christians see, in the Parable of the Patches and Wineskins, that the kingdom of God is present here and now in the lives of people who have responded to the message of Jesus.

Just as the new patch would not suit the torn old garment and the new wine would burst the old wineskins, so the kingdom of God must call for a new understanding of the message of Jesus for peoples' lives.

The Parable of the Sower (4:1–9 and 13–20)

The Parable of the Sower is one of the most well known of all the parables. The seed falls on four different types of soil: the footpath, rocky ground, among thistles and on fertile soil. At first sight this may be seen as careless farming. The thistles seem to be the result of bad farming. Surely they should have been dug out and burnt, not just cut down. This is, however, looking at the agricultural method used 2000 years ago from our modern standpoint. This is not the best way to understand the parable. The parable only makes sense seen against the agricultural system followed in Palestine at that time. Certainly some seed was wasted but this is exactly what used to happen. The sowing was done before the ploughing.

Meaning
A few verses later, after the account of the parable, Mark gives an allegorical meaning (4:13–20). But what would the interpretation be if that allegorical answer was not printed for all to see. There would be a simple parable, which shows, on the one hand, the many frustrations to which the sower's labour is liable; the fallow land with its weeds, greedy birds and rocky ground; and on the other hand, in contrast to this, a picture of a ripening field bearing a rich harvest. The meaning of this simple story is that the kingdom of God will be successful in spite of all frustrations and difficulties. Its growth is certain.

The allegorical interpretation of the parable is given in the Gospel. The allegory is all about the differing kinds of soil.

There are four such different kinds of soil representing four types of hearer of the message of Jesus.

1 *The unresponsive hearer*
   Satan carries off the word giving the person no chance to respond.
2 *The shallow hearer*
   The person who has no roots, lacking depth and persistence.
3 *The worldly hearer*
   The person who is seduced by the pleasures of the world.
4 *The responsive hearer*
   The person who, living a life of faith obtains depth, according to his faith.

There is something very unsatisfying about this explanation of the parable. Many scholars believe that this interpretation is not original and is not given by Jesus. It is believed that the interpretation is from a later period in the development of the Church and that it arises from using the parable for teaching purposes. Under self-examination a person is required to ask, 'What kind of soil am I?'. Such an interpretation misses the original and simple truth of the parable.

There is the third view that Mark himself is responsible for the allegory and that he uses it as a forecast of what is to happen in the rest of the Gospel. Certainly, the precise phrases used in the allegorical interpretation of the parable are mirrored in certain episodes in the rest of the Gospel.

(a) Those along the footpath are people in whom the word is sown, but no sooner have they heard it than Satan comes and carries off the word which has been sown in them *(4:15)*.

Later in the Gospel, Peter is on the way to Caesarea Philippi with Jesus and the other disciples. He has the word sown in him as he makes his profession of faith in Jesus in answer to the question.

'Who do you say I am?' Peter says 'you are the Messiah'.

Immediately afterwards Peter protests at the prediction of Jesus that the Son of Man will suffer and die. Jesus turns to Peter and says,

> Away with you, Satan. . .you think as men think,
> not as God thinks *(8:27–33)*.

The word, sown in Peter, has been taken away. The allegory
of the Sower has come true.

(b) It is the same with those who receive the seed on
rocky ground; as soon as they hear the word, they
accept it with joy, but it strikes no root in them;
they have no staying power; then, when there is
trouble or persecution on account of the word, they
fall away at once *(4:16–17)*.

This also will come true later in the Gospel. Trouble will
come as Judas and those with him seek to arrest Jesus in
the Garden of Gethsemane (14:43). The other eleven
disciples did 'fall away at once'. Mark records, at the
moment of arrest,

> Then the disciples all deserted him and ran
> away *(14:50)*.

(c) Others again receive the word among thistles; they
hear the word, but worldly cares and the false glamour
of wealth and all kinds of evil desire come in and choke
the word, and it proves barren *(4:18–19)*.

Again, this was to happen later in the Gospel. The rich
man, eager to find eternal life, hears the word but finds
he cannot accept the advice of Jesus:

> Go, sell everything you have, and give to the poor,
> and you will have riches in heaven; and come,
> follow me *(10:17–22)*.

He goes away sorrowful for he was very rich. The call to
discipleship was given but it was choked by his wealth.

(d) And there are those who receive the seed in good
soil; they hear the word and welcome it; and they
bear fruit thirtyfold, sixtyfold, or a hundredfold
(4:20).

This does not happen later in the Gospel. No one in the
Gospel story achieves this standard of discipleship. The
disciples desert; the women run away from the tomb at
the moment of resurrection in fear. The Gospel seems to
end on a note of despair (see chapter 9). Mark is writing

of the future beyond the Gospel; beyond the stark ending. He is looking to the period of the early Church where people hear the word, respond, and are willing to die for their faith.

The meaning of the parable for today

The Parable of the Sower is still relevant today. There have been many times in history when Christianity has faced extreme difficulty. Sometimes it has been persecution or suppression. At other times it has been treated with apathy. Throughout, the kingdom of God has not only survived but flourished. Christians of all nations and of every colour and race have found that their faith in Christ is the centre of their lives.

The allegorical interpretation of the parable also continues to have meaning today. Even if the comparison of people with different types of soil seems strange or even forced in today's world, the idea of examining one's own faith is a good one. Christians need to reflect from time to time on their faith, knowing that it is easy to be distracted from their calling to be disciples.

The Parable of the Lamp (4:21–25)

A lamp is not hidden under a tub or bed. The only purpose for a lamp is for it to give out light to illuminate the darkness.

Meaning
These verses are a comment on hearing and learning. Hearing is meant to lead to understanding: to hear without understanding is like lighting a lamp and putting it under a bucket so that it goes out again. To hear and understand without responding in obedience is to lose what you hear. Nothing is gained. Only the one who is obedient will keep what he is given.

The parable is a criticism of Jewish teachers who have hidden the kingdom of God instead of revealing it to the people. These verses owe their place in the chapter on parables to Mark. They are a group of isolated sayings and we do not know their original settings. It is, therefore, impossible to be sure what Jesus meant by them when they were first told.

The meaning of the parable for today

All Christians would testify to the modern day relevance of the Parable of the Lamp. They are able to point to the lives of famous Christian men and women whose lives have shone with the light of Christ. What is perhaps even more important is that they would also be able to name thousands of unknown and ordinary people, who, by their kindness, advice and example, have shown what it means to be a Christian.

The Parable of the Seed Growing Secretly (4:26–29)

This simple story is taken from everyday life. The seed is sown but growth to fruition is a mystery. All that there remains to do is to gather the harvest.

Meaning
The kingdom of God is like the seed. It develops secretly inside a person.

The kingdom of God is like the process of growth. It is the action of God. The same meaning is to be found in the letter of St Paul to the church in Corinth, when he says, 'I planted the seed, and Apollos watered it; but God made it grow. Thus it is not the gardeners with their planting and watering who count, but God, who makes it grow' (1 Corinthians 3:6–7). So the kingdom of God will grow by the power of God.

The meaning of the parable for today

There is little doubt in the minds of many Christians that the Parable of the Seed Growing Secretly holds one of the main truths of the Christian faith. No one knows how the kingdom of God grows in a person's heart. People cannot acquire it, buy it, or demand it. They receive it as a gift of God (this is called grace) and allow him to change their lives. It is by the grace of God that the kingdom grows.

The Parable of the Mustard Seed (4:30–32)

This parable is, in many ways, the simplest of all the parables.

The mustard seed is the smallest seed of all but when it is planted, it grows taller than all other plants. The mustard seed is not the same as that grown in Britain today as a salad, like mustard and cress. In Palestine, it is a seed that produces a shrub about eight to ten feet tall with branches strong enough to support and give shelter to birds.

Meaning
It is exactly the same with the kingdom of God. From the small beginning of Jesus announcing the kingdom it will grow into a vast kingdom of God.

This was a common metaphor for a great kingdom to be established by the Messiah. Jesus gathered a small band of followers, and through God's power, they were to become the people of God in the kingdom of God.

The meaning of the parable for today

The Parable of the Mustard Seed can be seen as indicating the process of being fulfilled. From the beginnings of Christianity in the first century the movement has continued to spread until it now embraces every continent on earth. From these small beginnings it has grown into something large. Christians believe the growth will continue until the daily prayer which Jesus taught his disciples becomes a reality. 'Your kingdom come! Your will be done on earth as it is in heaven'.

The Parable of the Wicked Husbandmen (12:1–12) (also known as The Tenants)

This is one of the best examples of allegory in the Gospels. The parable is based on Isaiah 5:1–7 where there is an Old Testament 'parable' about a vineyard that yielded only wild grapes. This signified the faithlessness of Israel.

Meaning
This allegory has obviously been developed in the period of the oral tradition by the early Church to show what is known as 'salvation history'. Salvation history is the story of God and his people and how God, since creation, has attempted to reconcile them to himself. The allegory is easily understood using the following key:

the owner of the vineyard ....God
the vineyard ....Israel
the tenants ....Jewish leaders
the servants ....the prophets
the son ....Jesus
the killing of the son ....the Crucifixion

others ....Gentiles
the stone ....the resurrection
                                       of Jesus

Verses 10–11 are not part of the original story; they record a saying used by the early Church to indicate the Resurrection. Jesus, rejected by the Jews, rises to become the keystone of the faith. The saying was included here to complete the full story of salvation history because to end with the killing of the Son would have been incomplete.

Jesus' audience, however, would not have recognised the 'son' as Jesus because they would not have realised that he was going to die. There must have been, therefore, another meaning of the parable before it was developed into an allegory.

The parable is a true to life description of a Galilean peasant's attitude towards the foreign landlords of which there were many. This parable may refer to the fact that in Jesus' time the Zealots (this was the name given to nationalists) were stirring up the peasants to revolt against such landlords.

The fact that the owner of the vineyard is living abroad is the key to understanding the parable. The tenants take liberties with the messengers because they know the owner is far away. The son's arrival makes the tenants assume the owner is dead and that the son has come to claim his inheritance.

According to Jewish law, if the property became ownerless then it became the property of the tenants. So they kill the son to acquire the vineyard.

The parable shows the depths to which the tenants will sink. Perhaps in this parable Jesus is criticising the Jewish leaders who, in their self-righteousness had not listened to God. They reject both God and his messengers. So the vineyard is given to others. Perhaps Jesus meant by this the 'outcasts' of Jewish society, although it is equally possible that he meant that God's message – the kingdom – was for everyone regardless of race.

The meaning of the parable for today

Jesus came to call all people to return to God. His own people, the Jews, rejected him. In the earliest period of Christianity the Church was very much influenced by Jewish culture and religion.

With the conversion and work of St Paul and his friends, however, the Church moved out and spread throughout the Roman empire. 'The vineyard was given to others'; to the Gentiles.

The allegory of the wicked husbandmen remains for Christians today the most superb summary of God's plan for the human race. They believe that God created the world and chose the Jews to be his tenants. They were to look after the vineyard of creation. From time to time they strayed away from God. He sent messages through the prophets calling for them to return to him but these were largely ignored. In the end he sent his son to make a final appeal for them to return to him. His son was rejected and put to death. But God refused to accept this rejection and raised Jesus from the dead. This death and resurrection of Jesus was for all men and women, not just the Jews, so that all might believe in him and through him, be reconciled to God.

SUMMARY

All the parables in Mark's Gospel are concerned with the kingdom of God.

- *The Parable of the Patches and the Parable of the Wineskins*
  The kingdom of God is new. It does not mix with the old. It is here now.

- *The Parable of the Sower*
  The kingdom of God will succeed in spite of all difficulties and frustrations.

- *The Parable of the Lamp*
  The kingdom of God is not hidden. It is visible for all to see.

- *The Parable of the Seed Growing Secretly*
  The kingdom of God grows by the power of God.

- *The Parable of the Mustard Seed*
  The kingdom of God will grow, from small beginnings, into something large.

- *The Parable of the Wicked Husbandmen*
  The kingdom of God will be taken from those who have misused and abused it and will be given to others.

Two of the parables have been turned into allegories. They are the Parable of the Sower and the Parable of the Wicked Husbandmen. The allegories may be the creation of the early Church and not Jesus. If so, the allegory of the Sower is a personal way of examining what sort of Christian a person is. The allegory of the Wicked Husbandmen is a scheme showing the process of salvation history.

In the case of the Sower, the allegory may be the creation of Mark himself. If so, it is a story pointing forward to important events in the Gospel.

Study Skills

Knowledge

1 What is a parable?
2 What is an allegory?
3 In the Parable of the Lamp, where does Jesus say the lamp should not be put?
4 What is a double parable?
5 In the Parable of the Wineskins what does Jesus advise not to do with new wine?
6 List the four types of ground in the Parable of the Sower. What happened to the seed in each case?
7 Which, according to Mark, is the smallest seed of all seeds on the earth?
8 How did the owner prepare the vineyard in the Parable of the Wicked Husbandmen?
9 What does the vineyard represent?
10 How is the resurrection included in the parable?

Understanding

11 What do you understand by the phrase 'the kingdom of God'? Explain how the parables show that this kingdom is both present and future.
12 What might Jesus have meant by the Parable of the Sower when he first told it? Explain the allegorical meaning that is given in Mark's Gospel.
13 Explain the meaning of the Parable of the Wicked Husbandmen.

Evaluation

14 Do you think it is easier to understand parables or allegories?

Illustrate your answer with examples from Mark's Gospel.

15 Write a modern parable showing one aspect of the kingdom of God for today.

Examination Practice

Describe briefly the parable Jesus told to the crowd by the lakeside while he was sitting in a boat on the Sea of Galilee.   (4)

What explanation does Jesus give of this parable to his disciples when they are alone?   (4)

Name two other parables in Mark which use the image of a seed or seeds.   (4)

Some people would claim that the parables are out of date. They have little to say to a modern world. What are your views? Give reasons for your answer.   (6)

All the parables in Mark teach about different aspects of the same subject. What is this subject?   (2)

Practical Work

● Design a poster or collage showing the parables of Mark's Gospel and their meanings.

4 The Miracles of Jesus in Mark's Gospel

The purpose of this chapter is to examine the miracle stories found in Mark's Gospel. It is important first of all, however, to look at some questions regarding the approach to this subject.

- What is a miracle?
- The miracle stories in Mark's Gospel.
- Why did Jesus heal people?
- The relationship between faith and miracle.
- What is faith?
- The healing miracles.
- The importance of the healing miracles for Christians today.
- Nature miracles.

What is a Miracle?

In the twentieth century a miracle is thought of as something extraordinary. It is seen as a direct intervention by God that breaks all the normal laws of nature. It is something that cannot be explained away. Because of this modern definition of miracles many people seem to think miracles do not happen very often today. They are regarded as belonging to an earlier age of superstition and ignorance.

The real meaning of the miracles will be missed if they are treated simply as 'newspaper reports'. The miracles are something much more important. They express the belief that the early Christians had in and about Jesus.

It must be remembered that the Gospel is an expression of Christian belief. Some Christians would say that the Gospel is not the source or proof of what happened. So with regard to the miracles, questions such as, 'Could this happen?' or 'What happened?' are not the questions to ask. The questions that must be asked about the miracles are:

- why did the Gospel writers include these stories?

– what did these stories mean to them?
– do these stories have any importance for Christians today?

The Miracle Stories in Mark's Gospel

Whereas there is no doubt that Jesus performed miracles during his ministry, many scholars would doubt whether the accounts in the Gospels are the reports of actual occurrences. In keeping with all the material of the Gospel, the miracle accounts have gone through two separate periods of development. The first is the period of oral tradition when the stories of Jesus were used and passed on by the Church. The second is the influence of the Gospel writers themselves.

WHY THE STORY WAS REMEMBERED

- The early Church used the miracles to express the belief that God was working among people through the Messiah.

- In this way the miracles show the developing faith of the early Church.

- This development is the result of using the miracle stories in preaching and teaching.

MARK'S USE OF THE STORY

- Mark is responsible for the order in which the material is presented in the Gospel.

- This order of material shows Mark's own belief. In other words the miracles are used by Mark to illustrate what Mark wants to say about Jesus.

SUMMARY

What observation can be made about the miracle stories in Mark's Gospel?
- It is impossible to discover the details of the actual events of the miracle accounts.
- The accounts, even though they are based in some cases on memory, are examples of the type of thing Jesus used to do.
- All the miracles of healing follow a set pattern.

  (a) Setting: description of illness, etc.
  (b) Cure: by command, touch, at a distance.
  (c) Crowd response: the reaction of the onlookers.

Why Did Jesus Heal People?

Many people would say that Jesus could not stop himself from healing people because of his overwhelming feeling of compassion and love for them. Certainly Christians believe that compassion and love are qualities that Jesus possessed. It should be noted, however, that there is only one miracle in Mark's Gospel where it states that Jesus healed out of a sense of compassion or pity (1:40–45).

The answer to the question, 'Why did Jesus heal?', can be found in one of the miracles itself. The woman who had a haemorrhage for twelve years and probably suffered from haemophilia, touched the cloak of Jesus believing that this was all she had to do to be healed. After the woman had admitted what she had done, Jesus said to her,

> My daughter, your faith has cured you. Go in peace. . . (5:34).

The older translations have at this point the words: 'Your faith has made you whole'. Jesus wished people to be 'whole', in body, mind and spirit.

Some Christians give the impression that Jesus is only concerned with their souls and their place in heaven but others believe that it is God's wish for people to enjoy wholeness of life, and anything that destroys that wholeness is contrary to the will of God. This is the real reason for the miracles of healing: to bring a wholeness of life to those in need.

The Relationship Between Faith and Miracle

Miracle and faith are closely connected. It is important, however, to understand exactly what the connection is between the two. Unfortunately, many people today see the miracles as events that make people believe. It is as if they are saying, 'We believe in Jesus because he proved who he was by working miracles'. The reverse is also true. Some people do not believe in Jesus because they do not believe in the miracles. They misunderstand the purpose of the miracles in thinking they are meant to bring about faith. Such people seem to connect miracle and faith like this:

MIRACLE → leading to → FAITH

This idea is not found in Mark's Gospel. It is not what most Christians believe. Christians of every age believe in Jesus because of the resurrection not because he performed miracles.

The connection between miracles and faith is quite simple. It is the opposite of what many people think today. Faith comes *before* the miracle. The connection between faith and miracle is

FAITH → leading to → MIRACLE

This is the pattern found in Mark's Gospel.

What is Faith?

Once again, this needs to be clearly stated. Many people seem to have an understanding of faith which borders on superstition. To them Jesus is someone with special powers, almost like an hypnotist, who could place inside a person the belief that they could be healed and therefore show faith.

Such a viewpoint is not found in the miracles of the Gospel. Faith is seen in the Gospel as an act of trust by which a person relies not on himself but on Jesus. It is an energetic seeking after the power of God, in the firm belief that He can do something for them through Jesus.

Faith in Mark's Gospel has two main characteristics:

1   it is an *active faith*; a belief that something needs to be
    done and can be done by this man Jesus. This belief
    shows itself in *action*:
    e.g. in the cure of the paralysed man his friends brought
        him to Jesus (2:1–12);
2   it is a *praying faith*; in the sense of a plea or request. It is
    a faith that believes it has only to ask in order to receive:
    e.g. in the cure of the leper the man asks Jesus to cure
        him (1:40–45).

Faith is the request and miracle is the answer. It is always in
that order.

The Church and healing today

*The Christian Church still practises healing. Sometimes it is by
praying over the sick person. At other times it may be by
anointing the sick person with oil. The Church does this because
the will of Jesus is that all people should be whole in body, mind
and spirit. Faith is important. A person with faith prays for
healing in the belief that healing can take place. Sometimes a sick
person's friends show their faith in action such as taking a person
to a healing service or to some centre of healing such as Lourdes.
Faith coming before and bringing about healing is as real to many
Christians today as it was at the time of the Gospel.*

*The miracle stories in Mark's Gospel can be divided into two
main sections:*

– Healing miracles including exorcisms; and
– nature miracles.

Healing miracles

I   Exorcisms
  1   The Capernaum demoniac 1:21–28
  2   The Gerasene demoniac 5:1–20
  3   The Syro-Phoenician woman 7:24–30
  4   The epileptic boy 9:14–29

II   Miracles on the Sabbath
  5   Simon's mother-in-law 1:29–31
  6   The man with the withered hand 3:1–6

Nature miracles

Healing Miracles: I Exorcisms

An exorcism is the casting out of an evil spirit from a person.

It must be understood that our twentieth century idea of illness is different to that of New Testament times. Illness has either a physical or mental cause and shows itself in physical or mental symptoms. At the time of Jesus the cause of many illnesses would have been unknown. Some exorcisms, for example, describe conditions which today would be thought of as mental illness or in some cases, epilepsy. There is no suggestion that Christians today view mental illness or epilepsy as the result of being possessed by evil.

It would be foolish, however, to dismiss evil altogether. Many Christians believe that it is possible for a person to be possessed by a force contrary to good; a force called evil.

I 1 The Capernaum Demoniac (1:21–28)

The first miracle recorded by Mark is the casting out of an evil spirit by a direct command.

'Be silent', he said, 'and come out of him' *(1:25)*.

The Jews of Jesus' day believed there were millions of

demons about who could possess people, causing illnesses of mind and body and tempting them to sin. Jesus faces such evil and by the authority he has, commands the evil spirits to go, and they flee.

Why the Story was Remembered

This miracle is remembered by the early Church because it contains the title 'Holy One of God'. The evil spirits recognised Jesus. That is why they called out

> What do you want with us. . .Have you come to destroy us? (1:24).

The title 'Holy One of God' is found only in this passage in the Gospel of Mark. It is a Messianic title. It means that Jesus is seen as belonging to God in a special way. He is the Messiah. (See chapter 2.)

The evil spirit says 'Have you come to destroy us?'. This suggests that there was more than one. Perhaps this one representative speaks for all the evil spirits. They are all faced with the power of God in Jesus who has come to destroy them.

Mark's Use of the Story

Mark claims that all the people were astonished as they witnessed this contest between good and evil. What is surprising is the comment of the crowd.

> What is this? A new kind of teaching! (1:27).

It is obvious, in this first miracle, that Mark makes no distinction between 'teaching' (1:21, 22, 27), 'healing' (1:25, 32–34) and 'preaching' (1:35–39). All three are part of one and the same mission to offer the kingdom of God to all people. Mark claims that all this is possible because of the *authority* of Jesus.

> He speaks with authority. When he gives orders,
> even the unclean spirits submit (1:27).

This authority comes from God.

As far as the structure of the Gospel is concerned, it would seem that Mark's purpose in the opening chapter is to show that:

1   Jesus is baptised with the Spirit of God (1:9–11);
2   Jesus wins the battle against temptation (1:12–13); and

3   Jesus wins the first round in the battle against evil
    (1:21–28).

I 2 The Gerasene Demoniac (5:1–20)

The place where this exorcism took place differs according to
the various translations of the Gospel. There are three
alternatives: Gerasene, Gergesene or Gadarene. They are all
intended to be the same place: in Gentile country across the
Sea of Galilee.

The symptoms of being possessed by an evil spirit are
described in detail: an interest in death; abnormal physical
strength; insensitivity to pain; and the refusal to wear
clothes.

Why the Story was Remembered
A poor man believed himself to be possessed by many
devils. His name was Legion. A Roman legion consisted of
6000 men. Legion was very strong. As Mark says,

> He could no longer be controlled; even chains were
> useless, he had often been fettered and chained up,
> but he had snapped his chains and broken the
> fetters. No one was strong enough to master
> him *(5:3–4)*.

Yet soon afterwards he sat at the feet of Jesus

clothed and in his right mind *(5:15)*.

Once again evil is powerless when faced with God acting
through Jesus.

The miracle is remembered by the early Church because it
uses another rare Messianic title: 'Son of the Most High
God'. Jesus as Messiah is the 'Son of the Most High God'
and as such has power over evil.

One strange feature of the account is the conversation
between Jesus and Legion. The evil spirits asked permission
to go into the pigs that were nearby. They were given
permission and were destroyed as the herd of pigs drowned
in the lake. What the early Church believed about this is
quite clear. Jesus was concerned to free a human life from
the power of Satan, whatever the cost. One human life was
more important than a whole herd of pigs.

Mark's Use of the Story
This miracle is placed by Mark just after the chapter on

parables in which the secrets of the kingdom of God are given to the disciples. That chapter ends with the calming of the storm where the first hint of 'failure' on the part of the disciples is found. It is interesting that the story of Legion ends on a note of discipleship. Legion wished to be a disciple but Jesus told him to remain where he was in his own district and tell all the people what

> . . .the Lord in his mercy has done for you *(5:19)*.

In this sense Legion was the first missionary figure in the Gospel.

A MODERN DIFFICULTY

Some Christians today have difficulty with this story. Jesus seemed to have no respect for the livelihood of a Gentile pig farmer. He allowed the herd of pigs to be destroyed. There are three ways of explaining the difficulty:

1 to accept it as being a contest between good and evil (see above);
2 to treat the death of the pigs as a coincidence. The commotion caused them to stampede. It has nothing at all to do with the cure of Legion; and
3 to say that the death of the pigs did not take place on the same occasion at all and has nothing to do with the miracle. It only became connected with the miracle because both events took place in the same village.

I 3 The Syro-Phoenician Woman (7:24–30)

Jesus made one long journey into the north, outside Galilee. He went into the territory of Tyre, in the country called Phoenicia, which was in the Roman province of Syria. Even there it would seem that he was known because a woman came to him and asked him to drive out an unclean spirit from her daughter.

Jesus' reply to the request of the woman to cure her daughter seems very harsh and even rude.

> Let the children be satisfied first; it is not fair to
> take the children's bread and throw it to the dogs
> (7:27).

The term 'dog' was used by the Jews to describe the
Gentiles.

It has been suggested that Jesus did not mean 'dogs' in the
sense of an insult but household dogs who are the family
friends. This seems, however, to be a rather weak attempt to
soften the harshness of the saying. Other scholars have
suggested that Jesus did not make the comment about the
dogs. They claim it has been put in the story by the early
Church, during the period of the oral tradition, to show that
Jesus thought his mission was primarily for the Jews and not
the Gentiles. Certainly Luke, who is thought to be writing for
Gentiles, omits the story, probably out of respect for his
Gentile readers.

The ready reply of the woman,

> Sir, even the dogs under the table eat the children's
> scraps, (7:28),

shows Jesus that she has faith and her request is granted.
The girl is cured even though Jesus does not go to see her.

Why the Story was Remembered
The miracle was remembered by the early Church because of
the emphasis on faith. The miracle portrays Jesus as being
unwilling to help a Gentile but does so because of the great
faith shown by the woman. When a person has faith that
Jesus can do something for them, then all things are possible.

Mark's Use of the Story
Mark uses the story to introduce the fact that the message of
the Gospel is not only for the Jews but is for everyone
regardless of race. This idea is called universalism. In curing
a Gentile, Mark is stressing the fact that Jesus' power over
evil is not witnessed by Jews alone, but extends to all people.

I 4 The Epileptic Boy (9:14–29)

Although the disciples had been successful in casting out evil
spirits on their missionary tour (9:1ff.) they could not help in
this case. The symptoms described in this account seem to
show some form of epilepsy.

Why the Story was Remembered

This miracle was remembered because of its emphasis on faith. The disciples did not have sufficient faith to cast out the evil spirit. The conversation between the father of the boy and Jesus was on the subject of faith. Jesus had faith and this is contrasted with both the disciples and the father. The father had a little faith but not enough.

Once again, through faith Jesus was able to defeat Satan. The disciples and the father had not yet sufficient of this faith which was built on a relationship of prayer with God (9:29). This miracle was important to the early Church because it encouraged them in their faith in situations where faith was being tested.

Mark's Use of the Story

This miracle takes place in the central section of the Gospel (chapters 8–10) which is a construction by Mark on the themes of suffering, death and resurrection (see chapter 8). Connected with this theme is a secondary one about discipleship failure. The disciples failed to understand both who Jesus was and what discipleship was all about. So this account is used by Mark to criticise the disciples.

> What an unbelieving and perverse generation! How long shall I be with you? How long must I endure you? (9:19).

Study Skills

Knowledge

1 What is an exorcism?
2 Give an example of 'active' faith.
3 Give an example of 'praying' faith.
4 What did the man with the unclean spirit in the synagogue at Capernaum cry out?
5 How does Mark describe Legion's appearance and character?
6 What did Jesus tell Legion to do?
7 What did Jesus say was the reason why the disciples could not cast out the evil spirit from the epileptic boy?
8 In which miracle is Jesus called 'Holy One of God'?

Understanding

9 What did the early Church see as the relationship between faith and miracle?

10 How does our understanding of illness today differ from that at
the time of Jesus? Describe, briefly, two miracles that illustrate
this difference.

Evaluation

11 Why do you think the miracles were remembered by the early
Church and recorded by Mark?
12 Why do you think that people at the time of Jesus thought that
mental illness was caused by demonic possession? Do people
believe in possession by evil today?

II Miracles on the Sabbath

II 5 Simon's Mother-in-law (1:29–31)

This is a simple healing miracle. It happened on the Sabbath
but does not cause any controversy. It does not conform to
the usual pattern of miracle and does not show the
importance of faith.

Perhaps the only reason it forms part of the Christian
tradition is that it is Simon's mother-in-law. The Simon
mentioned in this story was most probably the disciple
known as Peter. Although Mark does not make it clear,
Matthew, in his Gospel, points out that this disciple, whose
given name is Simon, was nicknamed Peter by Jesus. The
name Peter means a rock (Matthew 16:17–18). It seems
natural that the story would be remembered by Simon and
passed on.

II 6 The Man with the Withered Hand (3:1–6)

The keeping of the Sabbath was extremely important to the
survival of the Jewish religion. Genesis tells how God had
created the world in six days and commanded that the
seventh should be a day of rest. No work could be done on
the Sabbath. Any threat to the Sabbath day was seen as a
threat to the Jewish faith as a whole and was bound to meet
with opposition.

In the story of the man with the withered hand Jesus
healed on the Sabbath day. This counted as work. The Jewish
law said no healing could take place on the Sabbath day
unless it was a matter of life and death. Any non-emergency
must wait until the Sabbath was over.

Jesus claimed the right to do any action on the Sabbath that was for the good of people. To heal on the Sabbath was part of that claim.

There is no mention of faith because faith is not an important truth in this narrative. What is important is that Jesus sees that blind obedience to the letter of the law is stopping a man from being healed.

Why the Story was Remembered
The Church remembered this miracle because of the great pronouncement of Jesus:

> Is it permitted to do good or to do evil on the
> Sabbath, to save life or to kill? (3:4).

'To do good' and 'to save life' are both seen as the actions of God. The well known phrase 'Jesus went about doing good' does not mean that Jesus was just a good man doing good deeds. It means that he was acting as the Messiah for 'to do good' is a messianic action. As the Messiah, Jesus is above the Jewish law (2:28).

Mark's Use of the Story
Mark places the miracle at the end of a section showing conflict between Jesus and the Jewish authorities.

1   Conflict regarding blasphemy (2:1–12).
2   Conflict regarding eating and drinking with sinners (2:15–17).
3   Conflict regarding fasting (2:18–22).
4   Conflict regarding Sabbath law (2:23–28).
5   Conflict regarding healing on the Sabbath (3:1–6).

The action of Jesus made the Pharisees and the Herodians furious. They had been waiting to see if Jesus would break the law. They began to plot to destroy him (3:6). The concluding sentence of the miracle is most probably an editorial comment by Mark himself. It is doubtful whether the Pharisees and the Herodians decided to destroy Jesus so early on in his ministry. The comment fits in with Mark's emphasis on the suffering and death of Jesus (see chapter 8).

III Miracles Showing Faith

III 7 The Leper (1:40–45)

The details of this event in the life of Jesus are scarce. We are not told why the leper was wandering around when it was normal, in Jewish society, for lepers to be separated from the rest of society. All that is recorded is a chance meeting between Jesus and a leper. It must be noted that leprosy was not just the twentieth century disease known by that name but covered many other skin complaints (see Leviticus 13). The Jewish law of separating all those suffering from leprosy from the rest of society was an attempt to stop the spread of contagious disease.

Why the Story was Remembered
Jesus broke the rules and touched the leper. In a moving sentence the account says,

> . . .Jesus stretched out his hand, touched him, and said,. . .'be clean again' *(1:41)*.

The leper had a 'praying faith' which expressed itself in a plea or request.

> If only you will you can cleanse me *(1:40)*.

Jesus told the leper to go and show himself to the priest and make an offering for his healing. This was the law. The priest was the only one who could declare a person to be healed from their leprosy.

Mark's Use of the Story
Mark uses this miracle in two ways:

1. Jesus is seen as being more powerful than the Jewish Law. The Law separated the outcasts from society. Jesus cured them. Illnesses such as leprosy are against God's will and must be defeated.
2. Mark sets this account in the section that shows Jesus' authority. This authority is God given. Jesus is the representative of God.

The message of the miracle for today

For Christians today, the curing of leprosy is not the most important point about this miracle. The story shows the deeper truth that Jesus comes to a person at the point of greatest need.

*The miracle expresses the belief in a God who reaches out and
'touches'; a God who can heal.*

III 8 The Paralysed Man (2:1–12)

Originally this miracle was one of faith. The faith, shown by
the friends of the paralysed man who carried the stretcher is
an active faith. The details about how they opened up the
roof and lowered the man down to the feet of Jesus are so
vivid that many scholars claim that the account has some
eyewitness details retained in the story. There are, however,
some difficulties in this miracle:

1   in no other passage in Mark's Gospel does Jesus claim to
    forgive sins; and
2   the claim to forgive sins is supported by the miracle.
    Elsewhere in the Gospel, Jesus avoids such claims.

Why the Story was Remembered
It has been suggested that verses 5b–11a are not part of the
original tradition from which this account is taken but are a
very early addition by the Church. Such a suggestion makes
sense when a comparison is made between the account with
and without the addition. The account is complete as a
simple miracle of healing (see below). The basic reasons for
this suggestion are:

1   the early Church believed Jesus was the 'Son of Man' (see
    chapter 2);
2   the early Church believed Jesus forgave sins;
3   The early Church believed miracles were a proof of who
    Jesus was; and
4   the early Church had to face the charge of blasphemy.
    This miracle showed that Jesus' claim to forgive sins was
    not blasphemous.

Mark's Use of the Story
Once again Mark sets this miracle in the section of the
Gospel that shows both conflict with Jewish leaders and the
authority Jesus has received from God. The

> Son of man has the right (authority) on earth to
> forgive sins *(2:10).*

The message of the miracle for today

*Christians see, in this miracle, the important truth that a person's
sins can be forgiven. This forgiveness is offered through Jesus. He*

2:1. When after some days he returned to Capernaum, the news went round that he was at home; 2. and such a crowd collected that the space in front of the door was not big enough to hold them. And while he was proclaiming the message to them, 3. a man was brought who was paralysed. Four men were carrying him, 4. but because of the crowd they could not get him near. So they opened up the roof over the place where Jesus was, and when they had broken through they lowered the stretcher on which the paralysed man was lying. 5. When Jesus saw their faith, he said to the paralysed man. . . 11b. 'I say to you, stand up, take your bed, and go home.' 12. And he got up, and at once took his stretcher and went out in full view of them all, so they were astonished and praised God. 'Never before,' they said, 'have we seen the like'.

5b. 'My son, your sins are forgiven'. 6. Now there were some lawyers sitting there and they thought to themselves, 7. 'Why does the fellow talk like that? This is blasphemy! Who but God alone can forgive sins?' 8. Jesus knew in his own mind that this was what they were thinking, and said to them, 'Why do you harbour thoughts like these? 9. Is it easier to say to this paralysed man, "Your sins are forgiven", or to say "Stand up, take your bed and walk?" 10. But to convince you that the Son of Man has the right on earth to forgive sins'. 11. He turned to the paralysed man. . .

has the authority from God to forgive sins. Christians believe that through forgiveness a person can become closer to God and to other people.

III 9 The Raising of Jairus' Daughter (5:21–24; 35–43)

Jesus had just returned from the country of the Gerasenes. In the crowd that surrounded him was a man called Jairus who was a ruler of one of the local synagogues (see chapter 1).

Jairus pleaded with Jesus to cure his little girl who was at home, dying. On the way to Jairus' house Jesus cured the woman with the haemorrhage (see the next page).

Before they arrived at Jairus' house they received a message saying that the daughter had died. Jesus told Jairus not to worry but to have faith. He took Peter, James and John into the house where the girl was surrounded with people crying and wailing in their distress. When Jesus said the girl was only sleeping they all laughed at him.

Turning them all out except the parents and the three disciples, he told the girl to get up. She got up immediately.

Why the Story was Remembered
Once again, faith is the key to this miracle. Jairus showed a praying faith in asking Jesus to help. He believed that help was possible from Jesus. When the message arrived that the child was dead, the message of Jesus was clear. This was a message not only to Jairus but to the whole Church.

>   Do not be afraid; only have faith *(5:36)*.

The Aramaic words 'Talitha cum', which means 'Get up, little child', are preserved in this story (see chapter 1). It is thought that the Christians of the early Church valued such phrases which had been spoken by Jesus and used them in their original Aramaic form.

Mark's Use of the Story
The main problem with this miracle is the question of whether or not Mark meant it as a healing or a raising from the dead miracle. Jesus said that the child was only asleep. Some people think that Jesus still meant death in the same sense that it might be used today that a person had 'fallen asleep' when they had died. It must be noted, however, that Jesus made a point of saying that:

>   The child is not dead *(5:39)*.

Whatever the interpretation, it is plain that both Mark and the early Church saw in this story an illustration of the power of God to raise the dead.

The message of the miracle for today

For Christians today, the message of the miracle is almost that of a parable. Death is not the end, Jesus has power over death and a new life comes after death.

III 10 The Woman with the Haemorrhage (5:25–34)

This miracle comes in the middle of the story of the raising from the dead of Jairus' daughter. The woman felt it was necessary to come to Jesus secretly because her illness made her 'unclean' according to the law. Jesus was aware of her touch even though the crowd were pressing all around him. The touch was the touch of faith. This is an unusual miracle. It is the only one where someone touched Jesus believing that this was all they had to do to be healed.

Why the Story was Remembered
It has already been stated that the miracle is important because it gives the clearest reason why Jesus healed. His wish was for a person to 'be made whole'.

Mark's Use of the Story
The Greek verb used in the phrase which is translated

> your faith has cured you. . . (5:34),

is the verb 'to save'. This verb is used in the Old Testament when it means the salvation of God for his people. Mark uses it in this miracle to show that the time of salvation has arrived in the person of Jesus. In him the spirit of God is at work.

The message of the miracle for today

As already stated at the beginning of this chapter, most Christians would claim that it is God's wish that people should enjoy wholeness of life. Anything that hinders this wholeness is against God's will. This wholeness of life covers body, mind and spirit. They believe that faith in Jesus makes a person 'whole'.

III 11 The Deaf and Dumb Man (7:31–37) and the Blind Man at Bethsaida (8:22–26)

These two miracles should be studied together because:

1 they are the only two stories which Mark alone records; and
2 they are very similar in form.

The first miracle takes place in Gentile country. Jesus had travelled through Phoenicia (see the healing of the Syro-Phoenician woman's daughter – 7:24–30) and was now in the region of the Ten Towns to the east of the river Jordan. This area was known as Decapolis.

A deaf and dumb man was brought to Jesus with the request that he laid his hand on him and cured him. Jesus did so by using spittle and touching the man's ears and tongue. He also used the Aramaic phrase 'ephphatha' which means 'be opened'. The man's hearing and speech were restored. The crowd responded as usual

> He even makes the deaf hear and the dumb speak (7:37).

The second miracle takes place at Bethsaida which is still in Gentile country, to the north of the Sea of Galilee in the territory governed by Herod Philip. It is very similar to the first miracle. Again Jesus uses spittle. What is distinctive about the story of the blind man at Bethsaida is that it is the only miracle where the cure takes place in two parts. The man saw partially and made the comment that he could see men that looked like trees. In other words his vision was still blurred. Only after Jesus laid his hands on the man's eyes a second time did he find that his sight was fully restored.

Why the Story was Remembered
It is difficult to understand why these miracles were remembered. In both Jesus used spittle to effect a cure. There is no emphasis on faith and Jesus is cast in the role of the wonder worker. His actions in using spittle and touching the tongue or eyes are similar to those contained in popular stories of the day. The other Evangelists omit both miracles, probably because they are so different to the others in the Gospel.

Mark's Use of the Miracle
Mark has used the story of the blind man at Bethsaida very carefully. It is placed in the introductory passage to the great central section of his Gospel in chapters 8–10 (see chapter 8).

This introduction begins with the disciples having no understanding at all (8:17). Then the miracle of the blind man takes place, a miracle in two parts where the man gradually sees. It is used by Mark to indicate that 'insight' or 'understanding' will finally happen. In the next scene, Peter shows that insight or full understanding is possible. When Jesus asks the disciples who they think he is, Peter proclaims, 'You are the Messiah' (8:29).

After the central section of the Gospel comes the healing of Bartimaeus (see below) where 'insight' is immediate and discipleship follows. Mark has used the miracle as a kind of parable.

III 12 Bartimaeus (10:46–52)

This is the last miracle in the Gospel. Jesus was on his way
to Jerusalem and had reached Jericho. It is here that
Bartimaeus, a blind beggar, sitting by the side of the road
cried out to be cured of his blindness.

Why the Story was Remembered
The Church remembered this miracle because of the use of a
rare title, 'Son of David'. This is a messianic title. What the
miracle is really saying is that the blind man recognises Jesus
as the Messiah.

Faith is shown in this miracle in the sense of a plea or
request. The cry of the blind man,

> Son of David, Jesus, have pity on me *(10:47)*,

shows a faith that persists even when he is told to be quiet
by the crowd.

Mark's Use of the Story
There are three important things to note about Mark's use of
this miracle.

(a) your faith has cured you *(10:52)*.

Once again Mark has used the greek verb 'to save'.
God's salvation is offered through Jesus.

(b) he. . .followed him on the road *(10:52)*.

The word 'disciple' in Greek means 'to follow'.
Bartimaeus became a disciple. This is the only miracle
(with the possible exception of the Gerasene demoniac)
where the person healed is known to have become a
disciple.

(c) Mark places this miracle at the end of the central
section of the Gospel. Part of the teaching of the central
section is to show how the disciples misunderstood the
reason Jesus had come (see chapter 8). So, with
Bartimaeus becoming a disciple Mark is trying to show
how, through faith, a person might come to understand
and see. If one has faith, then salvation is received and
discipleship follows.

– *faith* is the *insight*
– *salvation* is the *result*
– *discipleship* is the *way*

The message of the miracle for today

This is the experience of many Christians today. By faith they grow in understanding and insight. They draw near to God by the gift of his salvation and become disciples in their own lives.

The importance of the healing miracles for Christians today: Summary

The importance of the healing miracles for most Christians today is not simply the fact that Jesus performed them. As was stated at the beginning of the chapter, Christianity does not depend on a belief that Jesus worked miracles. Most Christians would take that for granted. The importance of the miracles is the teaching they give about Jesus to the modern Christian. They say something about the faith necessary for Christian belief in Jesus.

1   *Christians believe that Jesus is concerned about their needs and will reach out to 'touch' them and help them* – the leper *(1:40–45).*
2   *Christians believe that Jesus forgives their sins and that this is an important part of their relationship with him* – the paralysed man *(2:1–12).*
3   *Christians believe that God's wish is for all people to be complete in body, mind and spirit. Faith in Jesus can produce wholeness of life* – the woman with the haemorrhage *(5:25–34).*
4   *Christians believe that after death there is life. Death is not the end* – the raising of Jairus' daughter *(5:21–24; 35–43).*
5   *Christians believe that faith in Jesus leads to a deeper relationship with him which results in being disciples and following his way of life* – Bartimaeus *(10:46–52).*

Nature Miracles: IV Miracles controlling nature

Nature miracles are, for some people, the most difficult to accept. They seem to be against all the laws of nature. They are, however, the only miracles performed without an audience other than the disciples. (Even the Feeding of the 5000 seems to pass unnoticed by the crowds. There is no 'crowd response' at all.) It would seem, therefore, that the nature miracles come from an early disciple source. Whatever the original miracles were, there can be little doubt that the accounts, as recorded by Mark, have been developed from their first setting. They show the developing faith of the early Church in what he had come to do.

IV 13 The Calming of the Storm (4:35–41)

Sudden storms are quite common on the Sea of Galilee. They tend to subside as quickly as they arise. Standing behind this account is probably one such incident. The fact that Mark records a detail such as Jesus sleeping with his head on a cushion may indicate an eyewitness source.

Why the Story was Remembered
Scholars tend to interpret this miracle as an 'allegory'. In the early days of the Church, Christians suffered persecution and had to have great faith to survive the violent opposition they received. This miracle shows a picture of the Church. The boat is the Church and the storm is the persecution of the Church. Those who lose heart and cry out in despair are reminded that Jesus is in command and he will steer the little ship of the Church into calmer waters. In the meantime they must keep their faith.

Mark's Use of the Story
Mark treats the miracle almost like an exorcism. Jesus speaks to the wind and sea with words that are very similar to those used in speaking to evil spirits. In the Old Testament the sea was the symbol of chaos and evil, which could only be overcome by God. The question asked at the end of the miracle,

> Who can this be? Even the wind and the sea obey
> him *(4:41)*,

is left unanswered. The answer is obvious. Jesus, acting as God, is the one whom even the wind and sea obey. The story is similar to the ideas found in the Old Testament:

'So they cried to the Lord in their trouble,
and he brought them out of their distress.
The storm sank to a murmur
and the waves of the sea were stilled.
They were glad then that all was calm,
as he guided them to the harbour they desired'. (Psalm 107:28–30).

IV 14 The Feeding of the 5000 (6:30–44) and the Feeding of the 4000 (8:1–10)

Once again, it is believed that the disciples were the source of the miracle of the feeding of the 5000. There is an eyewitness comment about the grass being green. This may seem insignificant as, in Britain, the grass is almost always green. This is not so in Palestine, where, in high summer, the grass can be more yellow in colour. It is surprising that no crowd reaction to the miracle is given.

Some people have tried to explain away this miracle and suggested that the crowd merely shared what food they had with them. This sort of explanation completely misses the meaning of the story.

NOTE ON THE FEEDING OF THE 4000

- Mark does not say where this incident took place although it must have been near the Sea of Galilee as the miracle ends with Jesus and the disciples getting into a boat.
- The details of the story are more vague than that of the feeding of the 5000:
  1 the crowd have been with Jesus for three days;
  2 the disciples ask similar questions to those asked in the earlier miracle;
  3 Jesus asks the same question regarding how much food they had with them;
  4 the instructions to the crowds are the same in both cases;
  5 Jesus blesses the food in the same way in both cases; and
  6 the main difference is the number of people fed and the number of baskets of scraps remaining at the end.
- What is most peculiar is that the disciples do not remember the earlier occasion.
- The most sensible conclusion about this miracle is that it is another version of the same miracle as that already recorded when Jesus fed the 5000. What the Church understood by the miracle is the same in both cases.

- It has been suggested that Mark has recorded both accounts to show that both the Jews and Gentiles are offered salvation.

Why the Story was Remembered
The early Church, noting that this miracle took place in the wilderness, 'a lonely place', would have seen a parallel with the feeding of the children of Israel with manna in the wilderness of the Sinai desert. Just as God fed his children in the desert so now Jesus feeds his people in the 'lonely place'.

Also to early Christians the story may have been seen as an anticipation of the Last Supper. Jesus blessed and broke the bread (6:41). Certainly this is how St John interpreted the story in his Gospel some forty years later (John 6).

Mark's Use of the Story
Mark saw Jesus as the Messiah. The Jews believed the reign of the Messiah would begin with a banquet. In this miracle there is a picture of the Messiah feeding his people. Such a picture points to the great Messianic feast in the future. The Messiah offers salvation; a way into that banquet.

IV 15 The Walking on the Water (6:45–52)

Many scholars believe that this miracle has the same root as the calming of the storm. Certainly there are great similarities. It may well be the same story that has come down in two different strands of tradition.

Why the Story was Remembered
As with the calming of the storm, this miracle is an allegory of the early Church facing the problems of persecution. The Church is rowing hard against the mounting waves and winds of persecution and opposition, but is making little headway. It is at that moment that Jesus comes, not as a ghost but as himself, to save them and take away their fear.

Mark's Use of the Story
As in the calming of the storm, Mark saw the sea as being an evil power over which Jesus had control.

The real key to understanding this miracle, however, is in the use of the phrase

It is I *(6:50)*.

The Greek words are 'ego eimi' which is the Greek phrase for the Hebrew 'Yahweh', the divine name of God. Its meaning is 'I am'. Mark intends us to see Jesus in this divine sense, walking on the water as an example of divine authority. The story tells us who Mark believes Jesus to be. He is God.

SUMMARY

- The miracle accounts are not historical reports of what happened. They are 'summaries' of the type of thing Jesus used to do.
- Most of the miracles follow a set literary pattern.
- The miracle accounts have been developed both by the early Church and by Mark to say something important about Jesus.
- The early Church used miracles to teach who they believed Jesus was: *the Messiah.*
- Mark also uses the miracles to say who Jesus is but the way he arranges his accounts shows that he is also interested in the *authority* of Jesus; the *salvation* offered by Jesus and Jesus' *conquest* of evil.

Study Skills

Knowledge

1 Name a miracle from this section that shows 'active faith'.
2 Name a miracle from this section that shows 'praying faith'.
3 Where was Jesus when he cured the paralysed man?
4 What did Jesus say to the paralysed man that angered the Scribes?
5 In which miracle does Jesus touch the person he heals?
6 What Aramaic words did Jesus say to Jairus' daughter? How does Mark translate them?
7 In which miracle is Jesus called 'son of David'?
8 How did Jesus calm the storm?
9 Why were the disciples terrified when they saw Jesus walking on the water?
10 To whom did Jesus say, 'Your faith has cured you'?
11 In the account of the feeding of the 5000, why did Jesus have pity for the crowd?
12 Name one miracle that took place on the Sabbath.

Understanding

13 Name one difficulty which is presented by the miracle of the healing of the paralysed man. Suggest an answer to this difficulty.

14 Explain why nature miracles are, for some people, more difficult to believe than healing miracles.

Evaluation

15 'The miracles were recorded because they comment on the person and work of Jesus'. Do you think this is true? Give examples in your answer.

16 Do you think that the miracle stories such as the calming of the storm are of value in preaching the Christian message today? Give reasons for your answer.

Examination Practice

Describe briefly an incident when Jesus was criticised for healing a person. What had Jesus said or done that led to the criticism? (4)

Choose *one* incident where Jesus shows his power over evil forces. Describe the incident in your own words. (4)

The man called Legion recognised Jesus:

(a) What did he call Jesus? (2)
(b) What explanation is there for the man's ability to recognise Jesus? (2)

Some people believe that it is still possible to be possessed by evil spirits, but others do not. What are your views? Give reasons for your answer. (6)

Why did Mark include in his Gospel so many stories about the power of Jesus? (2)

Practical Work

● Produce a chart of the miracles in Mark. Make sure that the chart shows:

(a) the exorcisms;
(b) the healing miracles commenting on Sabbath law;
(c) the healing miracles commenting on faith; and
(d) the nature miracles.

Also record on the chart any 'pronouncements' Jesus makes in the miracles (see chapter 1).

5 Discipleship

The purpose of this chapter is to examine the meaning, cost and reward of discipleship. This can be discovered by examining the following.

– Stories of discipleship:

1 the call of the first disciples (1:16–20; 2:13–14);
2 the appointment of the twelve (3:13–19);
3 who are disciples? (3:31–35);
4 the mission of the twelve (6:7–13);
5 the cost of discipleship (8:34–38);
6 who is the greatest? (9:33–37; 10:35–45);
7 attitudes to other Christians (9:38–41); and
8 giving up possessions (10:17–31).

– Mark's view of discipleship.
– Why does Mark end his Gospel in this way?

Stories of Discipleship

The Call of the First Disciples (1:16–20; 2:13–14)

In the opening two chapters of the Gospel, Jesus calls five men to be his disciples. The first four are called by the lakeside in Galilee (1:16–20). They were fishermen. Simon and Andrew, his brother, were fishing while the other brothers, James and John, were mending their nets. Jesus told them to leave everything and follow him. He said to Simon and Andrew that they were to become

fishers of men *(1:17).*

This phrase comes from the prophet Jeremiah and means that the disciples are to bring people back to God.

The other disciple called by Jesus was Levi, the son of Alphaeus. He was a tax-collector who was at work in the custom house by the lakeside. Again Jesus told him to follow and Levi

rose and followed him *(2:13–14).*

The surprising thing about these accounts is the way in which the five men respond immediately to the call of Jesus.

There are two important points that Mark wishes to make:

1   Jesus has the authority to call these men in such a way that they respond immediately; and
2   Mark reminds his readers that discipleship makes a total demand. Some are called to leave everything and follow, regardless of the cost.

Discipleship today

This calling is still evident today. This is what the word 'vocation' means. People who have a vocation to the priesthood, ordained ministry or religious orders, are required to turn their back on personal wishes and commit themselves to God regardless of cost. For some, as in the Roman Catholic Church, this means taking a vow of celibacy; for some entering religious orders it means taking the vows of celibacy, poverty and obedience.

The question of vocation, however, can be more widely applied to the whole question of being a Christian. The Christian considers discipleship to be a vocation. Vocation, therefore, is expressed through the different aspects of life, for example, through marriage, work and relationships with others.

The Appointment of the Twelve (3:13–19)

The first turning point in the Gospel story comes at the end of the miracle of the cure of the man with the withered hand. The Pharisees and the Herodians planned to destroy Jesus (3:1–6). This prompted Jesus to go away, quietly, to the hills to be on his own with the disciples (3:13). It was here, that he appointed twelve special men from among the larger group of disciples.

THE DISCIPLES NAMED BY MARK (3:13–19)

To *some* he gives
new nicknames.

1 Simon:	given the nickname Peter which means rock.
2 James:	James and John, the sons of Zebedee,
3 John:	were given the nickname 'Boanerges' meaning 'sons of thunder'.
4 Andrew:	Simon's brother.
5 Philip.	

6 Bartholomew.

7 Matthew: this was probably Levi. Matthew's Gospel names him as Matthew the tax-collector.

8 Thomas.

9 James: the son of Alphaeus.

10 Thaddaeus.

11 Simon: a member of the Zealot party; that is, a nationalist or revolutionary who wished to fight against Rome.

12 Judas Iscariot: The name Iscariot may mean 'man from Kerioth' or it could be from the latin word 'sicarius' which means 'assassin' or 'Zealot'.

These twelve men are called to do three things:

1   to be Jesus' companions;
2   to preach; and
3   to cast out demons.

The twelve disciples stand for the twelve tribes of Israel as opposed to those who might be expected to represent Israel such as the Jewish leaders. These are the men who are now to be found in the company of Jesus and to whom he gives his authority.

Discipleship today

Some Christian Churches, notably the Roman Catholic Church, consider that the apostles are present today in the persons of their successors, the bishops of the Church. They would also claim that the Pope is the successor to St Peter, regarded as the first Pope. The Church of England would also claim this unbroken succession. Other Christian denominations such as the Methodist Church make no such claims regarding their ministers.

Once again, on a wider basis, the task of the Christian Church in discipleship is the same as it was at the time of Jesus. Christians believe the Church is the body of Christ and as such, the members of that body are called to be the companions of Jesus, to preach his message of repentance, faith and reconciliation and to continue to fight against evil.

Who are Disciples? (3:31–35)

Jesus and the disciples had gone into a house to eat but this proved impossible because of the crowds (3:20). Mark tells us that Jesus' family set out to take charge of him because they had heard the rumour that he had gone out of his mind (3:21). When they arrived they stayed outside the house and a message was sent in to Jesus telling him that his mother and brothers had arrived and were outside waiting to see him.

Jesus asked,

> Who is my mother? Who are my brothers?

Looking at his circle of friends, the disciples, Jesus said

> whoever does the will of God is my brother, my sister, my mother *(3:31–35)*.

The family stayed outside because they did not belong to the company of Jesus' followers. In order to belong to the 'family' of Jesus, one must belong to his company. A person must not stay outside but come in, belong and do the will of God.

Discipleship today

Christians believe that the Church is the family of God and that within that family all are brothers and sisters. As with any family, its fulfillment depends on the love, care and concern shown to each other by the different members. Unfortunately, as with any human family, there are sometimes quarrels, disputes and bitterness that divide and separate both churches and communities. The unifying factor, as Jesus said at the beginning, is to belong to the family, which means to do the will of God.

The Mission of the Twelve (6:7–13)

The twelve disciples are sent out by Jesus on missionary work. They were sent out in pairs, perhaps for their own safety.

They were to conduct their mission under strict conditions:

- they were to take nothing with them except a stick;
- they were not to take food with them;
- they were not to take a pack or bag;
- they were not to take any money;
- they were allowed to wear sandals but not to have a second coat;

– if they were made welcome by any family then they were to stay there until they left the district; and

– if they did not receive hospitality then they were to shake the dust off their feet as they left. This was a sign to show that the disciples had no time for them because they had rejected God.

The task they were given to do was threefold:

1 they were to preach repentance – this was how the mission of Jesus had begun;
2 they were to cast out devils; and
3 they were to anoint the sick with oil and cure them.

Discipleship today

In essence the mission of the Church remains the same as the mission of the twelve. Modern day disciples still go out to preach repentance. The missionary scene may well have changed in the twentieth century but the principle remains the same. All Christian churches still work throughout the world:

– caring for the sick;
– feeding the hungry;
– fighting against evil injustice in many countries; and
– preaching the message of repentance through medical, educational, social, agricultural and even political ways.

Christian organisations, such as Christian Aid, Cafod and many others carry on, in modern ways, using modern methods, the mission of the twelve.

The Cost of Discipleship (8:34–38)

Jesus gives a very clear indication of the cost of discipleship just after the first prediction of his suffering and death and the rebuke of Peter (8:27–33).

> Anyone who wishes to be a follower of mine must leave self behind; he must take up his cross, and come with me *(8:34)*.

Two thousand years after these words of Jesus were first spoken, there is a tendency to water down their meaning. It is important to understand what these words meant originally.

(a) **To leave self behind**. To leave self behind does not just mean denying oneself. It does not mean going without certain pleasures in life like so many people do, for example, in Lent. To leave self behind means to put oneself last in all things; to have no care about one's life, position or esteem; and to have no desire for rights or privileges except that of belonging to God.

(b) **To take up the cross**. Again many people have watered this saying down. They seem to equate the word 'cross' with a burden or anxiety. 'We all have our cross to bear' has become a modern day expression. To 'take up the cross' was a frightening expression to the Christians of the first century and to many since in every age. For many Christians of Mark's day, their fate was to die for Christ. Discipleship means being prepared to follow Jesus even to the point of death.

(c) **Come with me**. This command of Jesus' for all people to come with him only makes sense when put into the context of the teaching that immediately comes before it. Jesus has just stated that he had to go through great suffering; to be rejected by the Jewish leaders; and to be put to death and to rise again. The invitation to go with Jesus is an invitation to travel along the same road. Discipleship can involve suffering, rejection and death.

To those who do respond there will be a reward. Just as Jesus will rise from the dead after the suffering and death, so those who accept the challenge to become disciples will find life.

> Whoever cares for his own safety is lost; but if a man will let himself be lost for my sake and for the Gospel, that man is safe *(8:35)*.

The reverse is also true. Those who refuse the challenge to become disciples will find that Jesus does not recognise them as members of the community (8:38).

Discipleship today

Many Christians today, especially in the Western world, are not called on to bear suffering, rejection and death in their discipleship. Although it is important to realise that discipleship does still involve this sacrifice for some.

In our own century, thousands of Christians have suffered martyrdom for their faith. Hundreds of clergy and laity, both Roman Catholic and Protestant, lost their lives in the Germany of the Third Reich. Many have been killed in the political struggles of South America, in the missionary work in Africa, and are still persecuted in many communist countries.

The twentieth century has its own Christian martyrs: St Maximilian Kolbe, who exchanged places with a condemned Jew in the concentration camp and was starved along with his fellow inmates, before being fatally injected with carbolic acid; Dietrich Bonhoeffer, a minister of the Confessing Church of Germany, who was executed by the Nazis; and Archbishop Romero, gunned down when he was at a prayer meeting. For each martyr well known, there are thousands who are little remembered but who suffered death because they were disciples of Christ.

Who is the Greatest (9:33–37; 10:35–45)

There are two stories about seeking position and greatness in discipleship.

In the first Jesus and the disciples were on the way to Jerusalem. Jesus predicted, a second time, that he would be arrested, killed and would rise again after three days (9:30–31). Mark states that the disciples did not understand what Jesus meant and were afraid to ask him to explain (9:32). Instead they argued, as they walked along, about which of them was the greatest. Perhaps they had understood enough to get the impression that Jesus was not going to be with them long and therefore, one of them would have to assume leadership. Who would it be?

Jesus stopped at Capernaum and when they were settled for the night he began to teach them about the true nature of discipleship. Discipleship should not involve quarrelling about greatness. He taught them the difference between greatness and humility. The only way to greatness was to serve others.

If anyone wants to be first, he must make himself last of all and servant of all (9:35).

He used a little child as an example for the disciples to follow. The child was the weakest member of the community. To receive the weak and the humble, that is, a little child, was to receive not only Jesus himself, but also God.

The second story happened on the same journey to Jerusalem. The third prediction of Jesus' suffering and death gives Mark an opportunity to state that the disciples were afraid (10:32). They still did not understand what discipleship involved. James and John prove this by asking for the best seats in the coming kingdom. This time Jesus makes it very clear that there is to be a link between his suffering and theirs. If they want to share the glory they must also share the cup and the baptism. Both 'cup' and 'baptism' are symbols of suffering. Jesus told them that they would share the suffering but as to granting their request, that could only be done by God himself.

Not surprisingly, the other disciples were angry with James and John. Jesus called them together and attempted to teach them, yet again, the meaning of discipleship. To be a disciple means to follow the example of their master. He does not follow the pattern, so familiar in the world, where rulers

> 'lord it over their subjects' and 'great men make
> them feel the weight of their authority' *(10:42)*.

Jesus set the example of a servant who gives his life for his people (10:45). The Christian disciple must imitate the example of the master.

Discipleship today

This is still the calling of the Christian disciple. Sometimes the opposite seems to be the case. Some people point out that most established churches have a structure that seems to be a ranking of greatness and position. This structure is called by different names in different churches. In the episcopal churches there are the Holy Orders of bishop, priest and deacon. Amongst these are other less familiar titles which seem to support the idea of rank: such titles as cardinal, archbishop, canon, dean and vicar. In the non-conformist tradition, the titles are less universal but nevertheless still seem to indicate rank: moderator, president, chairman and superintendent. Finally there are the laity, some of whom also have titles such as church warden, steward and elder. It should be remembered that all these positions are not positions of greatness. They are positions of service. Some are called to the privilege of Holy Orders or Ministry in order that they may, in humility, be the servants of the Church. If this is not clearly visible, then it is the weakness of the men and women in these positions and not the positions themselves that are at fault. To serve in humility is the foundation of Christian discipleship for all and every single individual in the Christian Church.

Attitudes to Other Christians (9:38–41)

The disciple John complained to Jesus that a man who was not a member of the group had been casting out devils in his name. The disciples had tried to stop him.

It is doubtful if the origin of this story was at the time of Jesus himself. Jesus never required everyone to join the circle of the twelve or even the wider band of followers. He had, for example, told Legion to remain where he was in the country of the Gerasenes and tell everyone there what God had done for him (5:19).

The story seems to come from the period of the early Christian Church and shows the uneasiness in the Church about who did and who did not belong to it. The answer of Jesus is quite clear. Anyone who acts in the name of Jesus is on the side of Jesus by virtue of the fact of not being against him. Even the most insignificant action, like the giving of a cup of water to a follower of Christ, will not go unrewarded (9:41).

Discipleship today

The story has serious implications for the Christian Church today. John's attitude shows the danger of Christians being too concerned with their own church group and having nothing to do with those of another view. The passage teaches Christians not to be too narrowly concerned with their own viewpoints but to be tolerant and receptive to others. There have been periods of Christian history when this problem has arisen time and time again. What is Christian discipleship? Sometimes the emphasis is put on a strict ethical code of behaviour, or, perhaps, on a clear statement of faith. During some periods, the emphasis has been on the authority of the Apostles or the Church, while at other times it has been on a real social awareness of the needs of others. Discipleship embraces all these emphases. The problem begins when one group claims that its is the best or superior or even the only way. These verses are a warning against arrogance on the part of Christians. Discipleship demands a tolerance of others. As Jesus said,

For he who is not against us is on our side (9:40).

Giving up Possessions (10:17–31)

A stranger went to Jesus and asked the question,

> what must I do to win eternal life *(10:17)*.

Jesus reminded him of the Commandments, choosing the more practical ones in a somewhat random order, and the man replied that he had been obedient to these Commandments since childhood. He did not say this from any sense of pride and so Jesus warmed to him. He recognised that the man was sincere and possessed the qualities of goodness.

The only thing that this man needed was to become a follower of Jesus. As in the case of Peter, Andrew and the sons of Zebedee and Levi, the call is given, 'Follow me!' In this case, however, Jesus told the man what he must do in order to become a disciple. He must give up his considerable wealth and give it to the poor. The demand was too great for the man and he went away sad because he could not bring himself to renounce his wealth.

It is important to realise that Jesus is not teaching that each and every person who follows him must give up all he or she possesses in order to become a disciple. What he is saying is that discipleship is a matter of total commitment that involves demands. The demand may vary according to the person. Peter and the others had to give up the fishing boat and Levi his position as a tax collector. For some people it has been the giving up of a family, parents or friends. For others it has meant giving up the security of a home in order to serve Jesus in foreign countries as missionaries, priests or teachers. The sacrifices made by people to become disciples are endless.

Having said this, it must also be realised that the possession of riches presents a special problem. Jesus went on to say,

> How hard it will be for the wealthy to enter the kingdom of God *(10:23)*.

He gave a most peculiar illustration,

> It is easier for a camel to pass through the eye of a needle than for a rich man to enter the kingdom of God *(10:25)*.

This is a difficult saying. Some scholars have suggested that the original word was 'rope' not 'camel', as the words in Greek are very similar. Others have suggested that one of the small gates in Jerusalem was called the 'Needle Eye' through which a camel could only pass with some difficulty. Whatever the interpretation, Jesus is teaching that wealth can be a barrier to discipleship.

Discipleship today

The danger with wealth is that it can separate a person from God. The reason for this is that if a person becomes obsessed with riches then he has little time for God. Money takes the place of God. Again, it must be stated that this same teaching applies to many other things besides wealth and possessions.

The main teaching of this story is that discipleship involves a commitment which demands sacrifice. The story ends with Peter, speaking on behalf of the disciples, claiming that they have given up everything in order to follow Jesus (10:28). In return, Jesus gave a remarkable promise.

> There is no one who has given up home, brothers
> or sisters, mother, father or children, or land for my
> sake and the Gospel, who will not receive in this
> age a hundred times as much – houses, brothers and
> sisters, mothers and children, and land – and
> persecutions besides; and in the age to come eternal
> life (10:29–30).

What this means is that discipleship does not mean poverty. It means real life. One way, for example, that this promise can be fulfilled is in the fellowship the disciple finds in the Church, which is the family of God. The other side of the promise is also true. Discipleship can still be accompanied by persecution.

SUMMARY

- The word 'disciple' means a 'follower'.
- Some people are called to leave everything and follow Jesus regardless of cost. This calling is called a 'vocation'.
- A disciple is one who does the will of God.
- A disciple is one who puts himself last in all things.
- Discipleship means being prepared to follow Jesus.

This can involve suffering, rejection and death.
- The true disciple will be rewarded with eternal life.
- The nature of discipleship is not one of privilege or position but is one of humble service.
- A disciple must not be arrogant but tolerant and receptive to the views of others.
- A disciple must be aware of the danger of such obsessions as wealth and be single minded in discipleship.
- A disciple imitates the life of Christ.

Study Skills

Knowledge

1 What were the three purposes for which Jesus appointed the twelve disciples?
2 Which disciples were brothers?
3 What nickname did Jesus give to the sons of Zebedee?
4 What was the occupation of Levi?
5 Describe how Peter, Andrew, James and John were called to be disciples.
6 What were the twelve disciples sent out to do on their mission?
7 What did James and John ask Jesus to do for them?
8 What did the man need to do, who asked Jesus: 'What must I do to inherit eternal life?'

Understanding

9 Jesus said that the disciple must 'leave self behind; he must take up his cross, and come with me'. What do you understand Jesus to mean by these words?
10 What can be learnt from Mark's Gospel about the cost of discipleship?

Evaluation

11 Do you think it is possible to be a disciple today in the way Jesus intended? What are the dangers facing the disciple in the modern world?
12 What do you understand by the word 'vocation'? Do you think that it is true to say that all Christians have a vocation? If so, in what ways can vocation be expressed today?

Examination Practice

On the way to Jerusalem, a stranger came running up to Jesus and

asked him a question about eternal life. Tell the story of what
happened. (4)
The man was sad when he left Jesus. Why? (3)
Jesus talked about a camel going through the eye of a needle. What
did he mean? (3)
Peter said that the disciples had given up everything to follow
Jesus. What did Jesus say that they would receive? (3)
It is not possible to be both rich and a Christian.' What ideas
prompt people to make such a statement? What reasons are there
for and against the view that you cannot apply the teaching of
Jesus on riches to the twentieth century? (7)

Practical Work

- Write a brief account about any Christian who lost his or her
  life through being a disciple of Jesus.

Mark's View of Discipleship

Mark's Gospel, as well as being the story of Jesus, who is the
Christ, the Son of God (see chapter 2), is also the story of
discipleship. Mark's picture of discipleship, however, is one
that is unexpected for it casts the disciples in a harsh light. It
is a story of failure. A close examination of the Gospel
reveals a distinct pattern that can only be attributed to Mark.
The pattern is threefold:

1 a period of response by the disciples, even though they
   do not understand;
2 a period of misunderstanding and growing fear; and
3 a period of failure and desertion.

(a) **A period of response**. The story begins with the call of
the disciples, Peter, Andrew, James and John by the lake side
in Galilee. The command,

Come with me!

received an immediate response. They were to become

fishers of men *(1:16–20)*.

Their response was one of enthusiasm. They went to find
Jesus.

They are all looking for you *(1:37)*.

Levi joined the band of followers under the same compulsion
shown by the first four (2:13–14). The disciples, in those early

days, received the protection of Jesus as they were criticised for not following the Jewish law.

The twelve were appointed as companions with the commission to preach and cast out devils (3:13–19). They were the privileged ones to whom the secret of the kingdom of God was given (4:11); and to whom Jesus explained everything when they were alone (4:34).

The first hint of a changing attitude to the disciples comes in the story of the calming of the storm, where Jesus asked them,

> Why are you such cowards? Have you no faith even now? (4:35–41).

This was the first moment of disappointment. The call and response of the twelve, however, was still effective and the first period draws to a close with them being sent out on their missionary tour with the specific tasks of preaching repentance, casting out devils and anointing the sick with oil and curing them (6:7–13). On their return they reported to Jesus and were taken to a lonely place to rest. This was not, however, possible since the crowds followed them, resulting in the feeding of the 5000 with the loaves and fishes (6:30–44).

(b) **A period of misunderstanding and growing fear**. The second period begins immediately. The disciples were on their way back across the lake when Jesus came to them across the water. They were terrified and even after Jesus had reassured them with the words,

> 'Take heart! It is I; do not be afraid', Mark records, 'they were completely dumbfounded. . .their minds were closed' (6:45–52).

From now on, this closed mind attitude was to show itself time and time again. They did not understand who Jesus was or what he had come to do. Mark infers that the patience of Jesus was wearing thin.

> Are you as dull as the rest? (7:18).

The fiercest attack on the disciples was yet to come.

> Do you still not understand? Are your minds closed? You have eyes: can you not see? You have ears: can you not hear? Have you forgotten. . .Do you still not understand? (8:14–21).

Peter, after his inspired profession,

> You are the Messiah,

protested at the forecast of the death of Jesus and in the
hearing of the rest of the disciples, received the stern rebuke
which once again shows his misunderstanding:

> Away with you, Satan, you think as men think, not
> as God thinks *(8:30–33)*.

Completely bewildered by the experience of the
Transfiguration, Peter, James and John, accompanying Jesus,
rejoined the rest of the disciples only to find them locked in
argument with some Scribes. The argument was over the
failure of the disciples to heal the young epileptic demoniac.
Jesus turned on the disciples,

> What an unbelieving and perverse generation! How
> long shall I be with you? How long must I endure
> you? *(9:14–29)*.

Jesus predicted, for the second time, his future death and
resurrection. Mark says,

> ...they did not understand what he said, and were
> afraid to ask *(9:32)*.

Rather they began to discuss which of them was the most
important of the disciples.

This period of misunderstanding and growing fear rushed
to a climax. Mark tells how, as they were on the road going
to Jerusalem, the disciples

> ...were filled with awe, while those who followed
> behind were afraid *(10:32)*.

James and John misunderstand. They request power for
themselves (10:35ff.). This led to ill feeling among the other
disciples (10:42f.).

(c) **A period of failure and desertion**. The third period of
failure and desertion began with the decision of Judas
Iscariot to betray Jesus to the chief priests in return for
money (14:10–11).

> I tell you this: one of you will betray me... *(14:18)*.

Peter boasted that he would never lose faith only to be warned of his forthcoming denial (14:26–31).

After the Last Supper the disciples did not really understand what was happening. They fell asleep three times in the Garden of Gethsemane as Jesus prayed in agony over the approaching and inevitable crisis (14:32–42). Judas arrived and greeted Jesus with the pre-arranged signal of the kiss. All was confusion as Jesus was arrested. It is at this moment that Mark records the chilling words:

> . . .the disciples all deserted him and ran
> away *(14:43–52)*.

Only Peter remained nearby, to find himself before long, cursing and swearing,

> I do not know this man you speak of *(14:71)*.

The cock crew, Peter remembered the words of Jesus and departed from the story of the Gospel in tears (14:66–72).

The desertion is complete. The tears of Peter herald the end and as far as the disciples are concerned, they have made their exit from the drama of Mark's Gospel. They do not re-appear in the story, even at the moment of resurrection. Their desertion and their failure are final. All that is left is the stark picture of discipleship failure.

This idea of failure is not quite finished. It is not only the disciples who fail. The women, Mary of Magdala and her companions, also fail. They witness the moment of crucifixion, note the location of the tomb at the burial, and are entrusted with the message of resurrection – a message to be given to the disciples (15:40–16:8). They fail to deliver the message and find no joy in the message of resurrection, only fear. They also run away and the Gospel seemingly ends in despair (16:8). Discipleship has failed.

Why Does Mark End His Gospel in this Way?

Why does Mark paint such a dark picture of discipleship? Many people have found it hard to believe that he did and have suggested that there is a lost ending to the Gospel (see chapter 9). There are, however, other answers.

Perhaps Mark has painted discipleship in this way in order to inform his readers that the way of discipleship is a hard and costly one.

Another reason may have to do with the very nature of discipleship. Disciples are not only followers but are also believers. What Mark is saying is that he will not give any proof that Jesus rose from the dead. He does not provide an ending that speaks of Jesus' triumph as the other Gospels do. There is no happy ending. What Mark does say is that Peter and the others are still Jesus' disciples. The message that is given to the women is for them.

> He is going on before you into Galilee; there you
> will see him (16:7).

In other words, Jesus is still their leader and they are still his disciples in spite of all their failure. His words are those of forgiveness. If they will only follow Jesus then they will see him. If they remain faithful then they will understand. This must have been a great comfort to the readers of Mark's Gospel. They were aware that Peter and the other disciples had come to a full understanding. They were also aware that they were in the same position themselves as they struggled with their own discipleship.

Discipleship today

Today, there are many Christians who value this view of discipleship given by Mark. They sometimes feel they do not understand the teaching of Jesus. They sometimes fail and desert. They have to come to terms with their faith in a modern world. They have not received the comfort of a resurrection appearance. Yet they continue to be disciples. They know they are disciples and believe they receive the forgiveness of Jesus for their shortcomings.

Study Skills

Knowledge

1 What did Jesus say to the disciples when he calmed the storm?
2 What did Jesus say to the disciples when they thought he was a ghost as he walked to them across the water?
3 What does Mark say about the reaction of the disciples to this event?

4 To whom did Jesus say: 'Away with you, Satan, you think as men think, not as God thinks'?

4 Which disciple boasted he would never desert Jesus?

6 What did the disciples do after Jesus was arrested?

7 Who betrayed Jesus?

8 Who denied that he knew Jesus?

Understanding

9 What do you understand about discipleship from Mark's Gospel?

10 'Mark's Gospel paints a picture of discipleship failure.' What do you understand this sentence to mean? Give reasons and examples for your answer.

Evaluation

11 Why do you think Mark paints a picture of discipleship failure in his Gospel?

12 Using evidence from Mark's Gospel, what do you think Peter was like in character? Would you have chosen him to be a disciple? Give reasons for your answer.

6 The New Way of Christianity

The purpose of this chapter is to examine the differences between the new way of Jesus and the Judaism of the Jewish leaders.

It is important to remember that Mark's Gospel shows the belief of the first century Christians. The views held about the Jews at that time are not necessarily the same as Christians hold today. The early Christians believed that Jesus had been sent by God to call the Jews back to himself. Instead of accepting the message of Jesus they rejected him.

It is not surprising, therefore, that there was some conflict between Jesus and the Jewish religious leaders. The Gospel comments clearly on this conflict as it outlines the new way of Jesus. (The background to the religious leaders of Judaism has already been set out in chapter 1.)

This chapter examines the following.

– The conflict between Jesus and the religious authorities:

1 blasphemy (2:1–12);
2 eating with sinners (2:13–17);
3 fasting (2:18–20);
4 working on the Sabbath (2:23–28);
5 healing on the Sabbath (3:1–6);
6 healing by the power of the devil (3:22–30);
7 ritual washing (7:1–23);
8 a question about divorce (10:2–12);
9 the question of authority (11:27–33);
10 the question of paying taxes (12:13–17);
11 the question about resurrection (12:18–27); and
12 the question about the greatest Commandment (12:28–34).

– The attitude of Jesus and the Pharisees to the law.

The Conflict Between Jesus and the Religious Authorities

Blasphemy (2:1–12)

This story is concerned with the healing of the paralysed man (See chapter 4).

Eating with Sinners (2:13–17)

The Problem
The Pharisees and Scribes would not eat with the ordinary people as they considered them to be irreligious. They would have nothing to do with recognised sinners such as 'tax-collectors' because they considered them to be immoral. Jesus had called Levi to be a disciple. Levi was a tax-collector who worked for the Romans. This was the main reason the Pharisees hated the tax-collectors. They were in the pay of the Romans. Levi, in gratitude, gave a party for Jesus and the other disciples, to which were invited a number of Levi's friends. The Scribes (i.e. Doctors of the Law) and Pharisees complained that Jesus was wrong to eat in such company. They believed it was wrong because Jesus was mixing with people who were not tolerated by strict Jews. Furthermore, Jesus was probably touching dishes and using utensils that were considered unclean.

The Reply of Jesus
Jesus' reply condemned the Pharisees and Scribes but also explained the purpose of his mission.

> It is not the healthy that need a doctor but the sick;
> I did not come to invite virtuous people but
> sinners *(2:17).*

If the Pharisees and Scribes thought themselves to be so perfect that they were not aware of their own sin then little could be done for them. The Pharisees considered themselves to be self-sufficient. They were not open to God. They were blind. They were outwardly religious but their hearts were far from God. Jesus said he came not for such virtuous people but to give hope to those who were aware of their need of God.

Fasting (2:18–20)

The Problem
Fasting was required from all Jews on the Day of Atonement (the day on which the Jews asked God, by means of sacrifice, for the forgiveness of sin) and on other special occasions such as severe drought or some national crisis. Apart from this, fasting was a personal and voluntary matter. The practice of fasting had grown up amongst the Pharisees as a sign of their superiority. They looked upon it as a practice

pleasing to God. By the time of Jesus, the Pharisees fasted on two days of the week, Monday and Thursday.

Jesus' disciples were criticised for not fasting. The fasting mentioned cannot have been the national fast on the Day of Atonement for all Jews kept this fast. It is most likely that it had to do with the extra fasts practised by the Pharisees and in this case the disciples of John the Baptist, who may have been mourning the death of their leader.

The Reply of Jesus

The reply of Jesus makes it clear that the time for fasting had not yet arrived. He used the illustration of the wedding. Nobody fasts at weddings. Jesus compared himself to the bridegroom. While he was still with them it was a time of celebration and joy. The idea of the wedding was taken up by the early Church as an illustration of the glory of the coming of God's kingdom at the end of time. They also saw the bridegroom as an allegorical symbol for Jesus in relation to the Church as the bride.

Jesus goes on to say that the time will come when the bridegroom will be taken away. This means that there will be time to fast after the death of Jesus in the sense that it will be, for a short while, a time of great sorrow.

Working on the Sabbath (2:23–28)

The Problem

The Sabbath laws of the Jews were based on the story of creation in Genesis. God created the world in six days and rested on the Sabbath. So the idea of keeping the Sabbath day holy was born.

By the time of Jesus this commandment had been developed into a list of 513 points of law with detailed conditions of each and every possible situation. The law stated, for example, that no work could be done on the Sabbath. Work was carefully defined under thirty-nine headings. Some of the things under the heading of work which was not allowed on the Sabbath were sowing, reaping, threshing, preparing food, spinning, putting out a fire, lighting a fire and carrying a burden such as carrying more ink than was necessary to write two letters of the alphabet or carrying oil, more than was necessary to anoint the little toe.

Jesus and his disciples were accused by the Pharisees of reaping, threshing and eating food prepared on the Sabbath day. All they had done was to pick ears of corn as they walked along, rub them in their hands and eat the grain.

The Reply of Jesus
Jesus in reply used a method of argument well known to the Jews. He referred to an old testament story in which King David, regarded by the Jews as their greatest king, had broken the law when it was necessary to feed his retreating and hungry troops. Jesus claimed that:

> The Sabbath was made for the sake of man and not man for the Sabbath (2:27).

In other words, human need is more important than Sabbath law. Jesus makes one further claim:

> The Son of Man is sovereign even over the Sabbath (2:28).

This saying shows that Jesus, as God's representative had the authority to break the Sabbath law.

Healing on the Sabbath (3:1–6)

This story is concerned with the cure of the man with the withered hand (see chapter 4).

Mark has grouped these five conflict stories at the beginning of his Gospel in order to show that Jesus is opposed to the religious authorities from the outset. Each story contains a different claim by Jesus that set himself against the religious leaders and pointed to the new way of Christianity.

1 ...the Son of Man has the right on earth to forgive sins (2:10).
2 I did not come to invite virtuous people, but sinners (2:17).
3 Can you expect the bridegroom's friends to fast while the bridegroom is with them? (2:19).
4 ...the Son of Man is sovereign even over the Sabbath (2:28).
5 Is it permitted to do good or to do evil on the Sabbath; to save life or to kill? (3:4).

The key to all five claims is the authority of Jesus. For

Mark and for Christians today, Jesus can claim these things because of who he is.

1   He has the authority of God to forgive sins.
2   He has come to bring sinners back to God.
3   His presence among people is one of joy like a bridegroom at a wedding.
4   He is not restricted by the limitations of the law, especially if he can 'do good' and 'save life'.

Interpretation for today

Sometimes Christianity is misunderstood today. Some people think of Christians as being like the Pharisees. They think Christians live by a strict set of rules and regulations. They see the Church as something negative; a group of Christians whose main cry is 'you must not do this and you must not do that'. They also accuse Christians of pretending to be morally superior and taking great delight in their virtue.

Many Christians would admit freely that, at times, the Church does give this impression, but they would stress that it is a false impression and has little to do with what Christianity is all about.

Christians believe that the message of Jesus is that every individual is of value to God and to each other. It is a positive message in which proper behaviour becomes a vital part of the relationship with God and with each other. This relationship is based on love. It is not a relationship in which rules are kept because of either fear or the belief that such actions will bring some reward.

Healing by the Power of the Devil (3:22–30)

The Problem
Jesus had just appointed his twelve companions (3:13–19). Large crowds followed Jesus although not all were sympathetic. Some people were saying that Jesus had gone mad and even his own family, having heard this, set out to

> ...take charge of him (3:21).

Some scribes had travelled north from Jerusalem. They were the strict Jews who were hostile to Jesus. Their criticism of Jesus was very harsh. They considered Jesus was able to cast out devils only because he, himself, was possessed by the devil. Beelzebub (sometimes Beelzebul) was originally the name of an ancient god of Syria but it had become, by the time of Jesus, a name used by the Jews for the devil.

The Reply of Jesus
In reply, Jesus used simple parables to show how illogical it was for Satan to cast himself out. If a kingdom is divided it cannot survive. It goes through a period of inner strife or even civil war. The same is true of a family. If a family is divided, then it is no longer a family in the true sense of the word. Again, if someone wishes to break into a strong man's house and rob him it would be better to tie up the strong man first. So, if Satan is casting out himself, he is divided

> ...and that is the end of him *(3:26)*.

Jesus finished his reply with a very difficult saying:

> ...whoever slanders the Holy Spirit can never be forgiven; he is guilty of eternal sin *(3:29)*.

Interpretation for today

This difficult saying needs to be understood correctly. Many people have lived in fear thinking they have committed this unforgivable sin. Perhaps what Jesus is really saying is that people who are aware of his extraordinary power in, for example, casting out devils, interpret that good power as something evil and fail to recognise God at work. A person who fails to recognise God, therefore, cannot receive the forgiveness of God. Forgiveness only works when it is both given and accepted. Many Christians interpret this saying as a warning for the person who would either refuse to recognise the goodness of God or would deny the very existence of God Himself.

Ritual Washing (7:1–23)

The Problem
Once again some Pharisees and Scribes had travelled from Judaea around Jerusalem to see Jesus. They noticed that some of the disciples ate their food with 'defiled' hands. The word 'defiled' means unclean in the sense of impure or contaminated. It was applied not just to the washing of hands but to vessels and utensils as well. The Pharisees took great care to wash their hands in a special ceremonial way, allowing an eggshell or a cup of water to run from the fingers to the elbow. They performed this ceremony as a sign that they were holy or consecrated to God. So, if they had, in the

course of the day, come into contact, however small, with Gentiles or even ordinary Jews, they would perform this action as a means of purification. The same rules applied to drinking and cooking vessels. Even today the strict Jew uses only his own special purified utensils.

The 'old-established tradition' (7:4) referred to by the Pharisees was a part of the 'oral law' and was additional to the Old Testament written Law of Moses. The Pharisees claimed these oral traditions had been handed down since the beginning. They were worked out by the Scribes and kept strictly by the Pharisees.

Mark's statement that all Jews obeyed this rule is an exaggeration. This did not come about until around 100 AD. By the time of Mark, however, many Jews other than Pharisees had begun to follow this practice.

The Reply of Jesus

The first part of Jesus' reply does not answer the criticism made but is a counter-attack against the Pharisees and Scribes. Quoting Isaiah the Prophet, Jesus claims that they pay only lip-service to God. They do not worship God properly but superficially. They put their own traditions before the Commandments of God. Jesus calls the Pharisees 'hypocrites'. This word is the Greek word for actor and so it became a word for someone who pretends to be better than he or she really is; someone who does not practise what he or she preaches. In this context in Mark it is used by Jesus as a criticism of the Pharisees who were outwardly religious but whose hearts were far from God.

Jesus then went on to attack the tradition of the Pharisees. He criticised such rules as ritual washing, calling them 'your tradition' (7:9) and stated that such traditions were contrary to the Ten Commandments which all Jews considered to be the basis of society.

He chose one example. The Commandment said 'Honour your father and mother'. To honour involves loving, respecting and, if necessary, caring for parents in a practical way. The Pharisees, however, had developed a practice called 'Corban'.

Corban was, originally, an Aramaic word meaning a gift. It had become used by the Pharisees to stand for something set apart or given to God. So a Pharisee might swear that his goods were dedicated to God and, therefore, it was not possible to use his money or possessions to help his parents. God did not benefit from this practice as handing over the money or possessions to the Temple treasury was not required. The practice of Corban was a device which provided a way round the Jewish law. It was an excuse to avoid caring in any practical way for parents. The law of Moses, the Ten Commandments, had been overturned by the oral law of the Scribes.

The rest of the section consists of a statement by Jesus to the crowd and an explanation of this statement to the disciples. The statement was not made on the same occasion but Mark includes it at this point because it deals with the general topic of defilement.

Jesus seems to be saying that nothing a person eats defiles or makes that person unclean. It is the inner thoughts of people that make them unclean.

There is some doubt as to whether or not Jesus really said this because in doing so he seems to be setting aside the food laws which were an important part of Judaism. Mark interprets Jesus' comment as meaning that all foods are clean (7:20). If Jesus said this and it was known to the early Christians, then why was it not accepted by the early Church who tried for a time to force the Jewish regulations on Gentile converts. Mark is perhaps writing with hindsight and expanding Jesus' teaching for his own day.

The disciples do not seem to understand and Jesus amplifies his teaching for them. He points to the digestive system of the human body. Food is taken in. It is taken to the stomach and the waste matter passes from the body. It has nothing to do with the heart. Jesus uses the word heart as being the seat or centre of the emotions in the same way as today a person may confess to love someone with 'all their heart'. He lists the evil thoughts that spring from inside a person and makes him or her unclean.

Fornication:	sexual intercourse between an unmarried man and unmarried woman. In New Testament times the word was often used in a more general sense to include prostitution and any kind of sexual immorality.
Theft:	the taking away of something belonging to another; stealing.

Murder:	the taking of a human life.
Adultery:	sexual intercourse in which one or both of the partners are married, but not to each other.
Ruthless greed:	a determination to obtain, at all costs, more than is necessary, without thought for others.
Malice:	an active ill will or hatred from one person against another.
Fraud:	an act of dishonesty against another to the advantage of self.
Indecency:	an act of outrageous conduct bordering on obscenity.
Envy:	to be jealous of another's gifts, abilities, good fortune or possessions.
Slander:	to bring, by gossip, a person into disgrace or disrepute.
Arrogance:	self-centredness or aggressive conceit in one's opinion of oneself.
Folly:	the foolishness of a person who lacks moral judgement; who interprets morality to suit personal desire.

Interpretation for today

The reason why these actions are wrong is the same today as it was at the time of Jesus. They are all things that abuse another person.

Christians believe that their faith is concerned with the value of human dignity and the worth of every human relationship. It has nothing to do with those things that use or abuse another person for one's own desire, profit or greed. Such things are wrong because they separate people from God and from each other.

A Question about Divorce (10:2–12)

The Problem

Mark does not state who asked the question about divorce but it was obviously asked as a test. It was an attempt to involve Jesus in an argument. The question was simple. 'Is it lawful for a man to divorce his wife?'

The Jewish law said that a man could divorce his wife if he found out something shameful about her, probably in the sense of immoral behaviour (Deuteronomy 24:1). At the time of Jesus there were two main schools of thought about what shameful behaviour meant:

1   the teaching of Rabbi Shammai, who said that the only cause for divorce was adultery; and
2   the teaching of Rabbi Hillel, who permitted divorce for any fault which the husband might find in the wife, even a trivial thing like burning the dinner.

The Reply of Jesus
Jesus replied, at the outset, by asking his questioners what Moses commanded. The reply was that Moses had permitted divorce. Jesus then went on to say that this was only because of the weakness of human nature. The purpose of marriage, according to the book of Genesis, was for the mutual companionship of one male and one female. Marriage means two people becoming one. This cannot be broken.

> They are one flesh. What God has joined together, man must not separate *(10:8–9)*.

The explanation given to the disciples when they were alone carries the argument one step further. Now Jesus is talking not simply about divorce but re-marriage. Jesus states quite simply and clearly that re-marriage involves adultery and is, therefore, against the moral law of God.

Interpretation for today

There is some disagreement amongst the Christian Churches today about their attitude to marriage and divorce.

All Christians would agree that marriage is for life; 'until death do us part'. In view of this life-long commitment, great care should be taken in preparing for marriage and efforts must always be made to support and counsel those who are experiencing problems in marriage.

Some Christians, notably those who are Roman Catholics, consider marriage to be a sacrament. In view of the vows taken in this sacramental celebration, such a marriage is, in the eyes of the Roman Catholic Church, for life and cannot be broken. Even if partners separate or the civil law grants them a divorce, they are still married in the eyes of the Church. Such a view takes the words of Jesus literally.

Most Christians who belong to the Protestant traditions take a different view. Whereas the vows are taken for life, it is

*recognised that marriage breakdown does take place. In
exceptional circumstances certain Churches will even allow the
re-marriage of divorcees.*

*Christians differ on the grounds on which divorce ought to be
allowed:*

1   *some would say that adultery should be the only reason;*
2   *some believe desertion is an acceptable reason; and*
3   *others would follow the civil law and consider irretrievable
    breakdown as the main grounds for the ending of a marriage.*

*All Christians who are sympathetic to divorce believe that such
a course of action should only be taken if there is no possibility
of forgiveness and reconciliation between the married partners.*

The Question of Authority (11:27–33)

Just as Mark collected together the five conflict stories at the
beginning of his Gospel (2:1 to 3:6), so he now shows the
mounting opposition found in Jerusalem.

The Problem
This is the first of a series of questions designed to trap Jesus
into saying something that could lead to his arrest. The
Jewish authorities had already taken the decision to do away
with him (11:18).

The first group to challenge Jesus were representatives of
the Sanhedrin. Mark calls them Priests, Scribes and Elders
(11:27). It was quite natural for them to challenge Jesus,
especially in view of his own challenge to their authority the
previous day, when he ordered out of the temple those who
had permission to trade there (11:15–18).

The question they asked Jesus was a trap.

Who gave you authority to act in this way *(11:28)*.

Whatever reply Jesus gave would have placed him in danger.
If he had said his authority was from God, he would have
laid himself open to a charge of blasphemy. If he had said he
was acting under his own authority, he would have been
subject to ridicule.

The Reply of Jesus
Jesus refused to answer. Instead, following a typical Jewish
method of debate, he asked them a question in return.

The baptism of John: was it from God or from
men? *(11:30)*.

The baptism of John was a phrase that summed up all John's work. He had called people to repent and baptised those who had responded. The questioners were now placed in the same difficulty as Jesus had been in. If they said John was an ordinary man they would make the ordinary people angry for they regarded John as a prophet and a prophet received his authority from God. If they said John received his authority from God then they would be criticised for not listening to him. In the end they refused to answer which allowed Jesus to refuse to answer as well.

It would be wrong to consider that Jesus had simply evaded the question. He is, in one sense, hinting at his own authority. He had been baptised by John and his authority stemmed from that moment.

> Thou art my Son, my beloved; on thee my favour rests (1:11).

The Question of Paying Taxes (12:13–17)

The Problem
The second question designed to trap Jesus follows a similar pattern to the first. This time it is the Pharisees and Herodians (see chapter 2) who ask the question.

> Are we or are we not permitted to pay taxes to the Roman Emperor? (12:14).

Once again Jesus was faced with the problem of answering. If he said 'Yes', he would have become unpopular with the people, who hated the tax. He would also have become even more unpopular than he already was with the Pharisees, who were bitterly opposed to the Roman occupation.

If he said 'No', he would be committing treason against Rome. He would also be offending the Herodians who gave their support to the Roman Emperor because it was he who had allowed the Herod dynasty to exercise power in Palestine.

The tax in question was a poll-tax imposed by the Romans in 6 AD. It was extremely unpopular because it was the symbol of Roman rule. The Roman coins also had the head and inscription of the Emperor on them. They belonged to him and were issued and used only by his authority.

The Reply of Jesus
Jesus' reply was to call for a coin and ask whose head and

inscription were to be found on it. When they said 'Caesar's' his comment was:

> Pay Caesar what is due to Caesar, and pay God
> what is due to God *(12:17).*

What Jesus meant by this answer was:

1   the Jews, by using Roman coins recognised the Romans as the state authority;
2   the Jews, therefore, must recognise civil authority; and
3   there was a further allegiance owing to God.

Interpretation for today

There have been tensions between Church and State throughout history. This story about the paying of taxes to Caesar seems to be at the very centre of the relationship.

Most Christians today would accept that the Church and State must exist side by side. The State has the right to make demands on Christians in such matters as taxes, but has no right to make demands that are contrary to the consciences of Christians. If there is a conflict between duty to the State and faithfulness to God, Christians would claim that God and his demands must come first.

The Question about Resurrection (12:18–27)

The Problem

The Sadducees are mentioned for the first time by name in Mark's gospel (see chapter 1). They asked a question about resurrection even though they themselves did not believe in any form of resurrection. They assumed Jesus held the current belief of many Jews, especially the Pharisees, that there would be some form of resurrection for those who had been faithful to God.

The question itself was based on an ancient Jewish law called the Levirate law (Deuteronomy 25:5–6). The purpose of this law, which was not widely practised at the time of Jesus, was to preserve both a family line and the inheritance of family possessions and property. The question asked of Jesus was over-emphasised to the point of being absurd.

There were seven brothers. The first married but died childless. The second, third, fourth and so on, each, in turn, married the widow and died childless. Finally, the widow, herself, died. Whose wife will she be at the resurrection?

The Reply of Jesus
Jesus' reply is in two distinct parts.

(a) **At the resurrection people do not marry**. They will be like
angels. What Jesus is saying is that there is no need for
marriage at the resurrection. Marriage is an earthly institution
which ends at death. This is made very clear in the rite of
marriage where a couple enter into marriage 'till death do us
part'.

(b) **Jesus then went on to teach the Sadducees that there was
to be a resurrection**. He claimed that it was implied in the
Scriptures. When God appeared to Moses at the time of the
burning bush, He told Moses, 'I am the God of Abraham, the
God of Isaac and the God of Jacob' (12:26). These three
Jewish leaders were long since dead but God still speaks of
them as living. He says 'I am' their God not 'I was' their
God. This indicates that they are still alive. 'God is not God
of the dead but of the living (12:27).

The Question about the Greatest Commandment (12:28–34)

The Problem
The Scribes were the Doctors of the Law (see chapter 1).
They studied the Scriptures in minute detail. In the written
law there were some 613 different commandments.
Technically, they were all equally important but it was
natural that debates took place as to their relative importance.
So Jesus was asked for his opinion. Which commandment
did he consider to be the greatest?

The Reply of Jesus
Jesus' reply is a quotation from the daily prayer of the Jews
called the Shema.

'Hear, O Israel: the Lord our God is the only Lord;/love the
Lord your God with all your heart,/with all your soul,/with
all your mind,/and with all your strength' (Deuteronomy
6:4–5).

The second quotation Jesus gave in answer was: 'Love your
neighbour as yourself (Leviticus 19:18). In Leviticus
'neighbour' meant 'Israelite' or 'fellow-countryman'. It is
probable from the Gospel that Jesus extended the thought to
cover anyone of any race.

For once, the Scribe does not oppose Jesus. In fact, he commends him. Love of God and one's neighbour is more valuable than sacrifice. In turn Jesus compliments the Scribe for his insight, saying he is not far from the kingdom of God.

Interpretation for today

All Christians today would join together in accepting these words of Jesus as the very centre of the Christian faith. To love God with all that the human being possesses and to love each other as much as oneself is the heart of Christianity.

The attitudes of Jesus and the Pharisees to the Law

Most Christians today, would understand the main differences in the attitudes of Jesus and the Pharisees to the Law as being:

- *at the time of Jesus, strict obedience to the Law was the way of the Pharisees;*
- *this strict attitude was applied to every part of life;*
- *the Scribes developed the law adding the oral law which catered for every eventuality;*
- *the Pharisees kept the law in its entirety because they wished to be absolutely obedient to God;*
- *Jesus seems, at first sight, to have little time for the law. This is not so. Jesus is not against obedience to the law but he is against obedience that simply follows the letter of the law. This is not full obedience. The heart of a person may not be in it;*
- *Jesus believed that a person's response to God must come from the heart. It is possible to obey the law but still disregard both God and other people. This is Jesus' main criticism of the way the Pharisees treat the law;*
- *the second reason Jesus criticised the way of the Pharisees is because their legalistic obedience leads them to place too much emphasis on their own achievements; this, in turn, leads to thoughts of reward and punishments;*

  Jesus believed that people should receive everything from God as a gift; there must be no thought of obeying to receive reward. The law helps in this. It is not a fence to restrict; it is not a system of rewards and punishments but a guide to how to return to God;

- *the way of Jesus is the harder way. For example, to keep the Sabbath out of sheer joy for God can be harder than mere abstinence from every kind of work; and*
- *the way of Jesus is an obedience in freedom not slavery. It comes from the heart. It is to this kind of obedience to the law that Jesus calls people by his teaching and his actions.*

Study Skills

Knowledge

1 Why was Jesus accused of being blasphemous when he healed the paralysed man?
2 What did Jesus say to the Scribes of the Pharisees' party when they criticised him for eating with sinners and tax-collectors in Levi's house?
3 How did the disciples break the Sabbath law when they were walking through the cornfields?
4 What did Jesus say when he was criticised for healing the man with the withered hand on the Sabbath?
5 Who was Beelzebub?
6 What was Corban?
7 Jesus says that the following evil thoughts come from within a person. What do they mean?
   Fornication; ruthless greed, and slander.
8 What did Jesus say when he was asked if it was permitted to pay taxes to Ceasar?
9 What was the Levirate law?
10 Which commandment did Jesus consider to be the greatest?

Understanding

11 Why do you think the Pharisees criticised Jesus for allowing his disciples to pluck ears of corn on the Sabbath? Give reasons for your answer.
12 What do you understand is new about Jesus' teaching on the subject of the Sabbath Law?
13 Jesus stated that 'evil things all come from inside, and they defile a man'. What do you understand Jesus to mean by these words? Give examples of the 'evil things' Jesus meant.

Evaluation

14 Choose one occasion when Jesus disagreed with the Pharisees. Give both sides of the argument and state which side you agree with and the reasons why.
15 How far do you think Jesus' teaching about divorce in Mark's

Gospel is still practical in a modern world? Give reasons for your answer.

Examination Practice

Describe what happened when a number of Pharisees and men of Herod's party were sent to trap Jesus over the question of paying taxes.   (5)

What was crafty about the question they asked?   (2)

Mention briefly another occasion when the religious leaders tried to trap Jesus.   (2)

What do you think Jesus meant by the statement, 'Pay Caesar what is due to Caesar'?   (5)

How far do you agree that Christians have a duty to the civil authority?   (6)

Practical Work

- Find out all you can about the Pharisees and Scribes. Present this information on large sheets of paper for display. Underline all the points on which Jesus came into conflict with the Pharisees and Scribes. Produce a section on the display in which the teaching of Jesus is shown.

7 The Sacraments in Mark's Gospel

The purpose of this chapter is to look at the meaning and origin of the two sacraments of baptism and the eucharist and assess their importance for Christians today. This can be discovered by examining the following.

- What is a sacrament?
- The account of the baptism in Mark.
- The meaning of baptism in Christian belief.
- Different names for the eucharist.
- The eucharist against the background of Passover.
- The account of the Last Supper in Mark.

What is a Sacrament?

Christians claim that a sacrament is a sign instituted by Jesus that gives people the grace of God, which is the free gift of salvation. Another definition is 'an outward and visible sign of an inward and spiritual grace'. Water, for example, is an 'outward and visible sign' that signifies baptism.

It is important to understand exactly what is meant by 'sign'. Signs are things which convey ideas. The action of smiling or weeping is a sign of a person's feelings. A flag is a sign of a nation. Written or spoken words are also signs. To say, 'I love you' is a sign that shows the feelings of one person for another. Sacraments are words and actions together that make up a sign. According to Christianity, however, the sacraments are not just signs to express ideas. They are real, in the sense that they make real what they stand for. They produce the very things they signify.

Christianity has always claimed that *Jesus is a sacrament.* He is a sign of God's wish to call the whole human race to himself. They would also claim that the *Church is a sacrament* because Jesus lives on in the life of the Church. Through the Church he is still active in the world. The sacraments themselves, are special ways in which Christ continues to do his work.

The Roman Catholic Church and the Eastern Orthodox Church recognise seven sacraments; baptism; confirmation; eucharist; penance; anointing the sick; holy orders; and

marriage. The Church of England and the other main
Protestant churches recognise only two as sacraments:
baptism and eucharist. The reason for this is that they claim
that only these two were instituted by Jesus himself. Even
though the Roman Catholic Church would dispute this and
claim that all seven were instituted by Jesus, this chapter is
concerned only with the sacraments of baptism and the
eucharist.

The Account of the Baptism in Mark (1:2–11)

Mark begins his Gospel with the account of the baptism of
Jesus. John the Baptist appeared in the wilderness of Judaea
preaching a

> . . .baptism in token of repentance, for the
> forgiveness of sins (1:4).

He drew great crowds to the River Jordan, a strange
prophetic figure in his

> '. . .rough coat of camel's hair' and eating 'locusts
> and wild honey' (1:6).

People from all around the 'Judaean countryside' and from
'Jerusalem' went out to see him (1:5).
   The content of the preaching and the baptism John offered
was a call to the people to prepare themselves for the coming
of the Messiah.

> After me comes one who is mightier than I. I am
> not fit to unfasten his shoes. I have baptised you
> with water; he will baptise you with the Holy
> Spirit (1:7–8).

John's baptism was one of water, and as such would not
have been uncommon to the Jews who understood baptism
in terms of an experience of purification and renewal.
Baptism was even used along with circumcision as an
initiation into Judaism by converts. It is doubtful if this was
the meaning behind John's use of the act. His understanding
of baptism was one of forgiveness for the person who
repented and became one of the expectant forward looking
community awaiting the arrival of the Christ.

Into such an atmosphere, among the gathering crowds around John, came Jesus from Nazareth in Galilee and he himself was baptised in the Jordan by John.

One of the most difficult questions concerning the baptism of Jesus is: Why did Jesus need to be baptised into a baptism of repentance for the forgiveness of sins if he was, as Christians believe, sinless? There have been many attempts to answer this question.

1 The first is completely unacceptable, as far as Christians are concerned, and that is that Jesus was a sinner.
2 It has been suggested that Jesus was 'play-acting' in an attempt to identify himself with John the Baptist's role as a 'preparer' of the way. Again, most Christians would reject the idea of Jesus pretending to be a sinner.
3 Some people have suggested that Jesus, by being baptised, was showing great humility in undergoing the act without any need to do so.
4 The key to the reason why Jesus was baptised might lie in the words spoken by the 'voice from heaven'. The expression 'voice from heaven' (1:11) is an Old Testament way of saying the 'voice of God'.

Thou art my Son, my Beloved; on thee my favour rests *(1:11)*.

These words are a combination of two Old Testament texts.

The first comes from a psalm of the king on whom sonship is conferred by God. As 'son' of God he has a part to play in the rule of God on earth. Such is the part to be played by the Messiah.

'"You are my son" he said:/"this day I became your father/ Ask of me what you will:/I will give you the nations as your inheritance,/the ends of the earth as your possession"' (Psalm 2.7).

The message of God is, therefore, that Jesus is the 'Son of God'; the Messiah.

The second text in God's message at the baptism of Jesus indicates the type of Messiah Jesus was to be. He was not to be the popular image of the one who would drive the Romans out. He was to be a servant. 'Here is my servant, whom I uphold,/my chosen one in whom I delight' (Isaiah 42:1).

The second quotation comes from the prophet Isaiah, who in four songs about the servant, tells of him suffering and dying to bring the people back to God, their sins forgiven. There is remarkable similarity between the experience forecast for the 'suffering servant' of Isaiah and the experience of Jesus (see chapter 8). (The four songs of Isaiah can be found in Isaiah 42:1–9; 49:1–6; 50:4–9; 52:13 to 53:12.) The baptism of Jesus is the moment God confirms him as the Messiah.

The meaning of Baptism in Christian belief

Baptism by water
Mark says that baptism is by water. In the Bible, water is symbolic of two ideas.

(a) **Water is *life*** (i.e. salvation). As far back as the myth of creation in Genesis water stands for life. The garden of Eden was supplied with water by the flow of four streams (Genesis 2:10). The might of God is seen in His saving acts regarding water. He divided the waters of the sea through which the Israelites made their escape (Exodus 14:21–30). He produces life-giving water for Israel in their desert wanderings (Exodus 15:23–25). Both the prophets and the Psalms use the symbol of water to represent life in the sense of the salvation of God (Psalm 22:1–3; Isaiah 41:18; 44:3; Jeremiah 2:13). In John's Gospel, Jesus also uses the symbolism of water in offering eternal life (John 4:14).

(b) **Water is *suffering* and *death***. The imagery of water appears also in opposite terms standing for suffering and death. This symbolism is behind the ancient story of the flood in which God destroys his creation to begin again with faithful Noah and his family (Genesis 6:5–8:22). The Psalmist uses the same imagery in terms of personal distress (Psalm 69:3–16).

Jesus himself uses this image of water as suffering. James and John ask Jesus if they may have the place of honour on the right and left hand in his glory. Jesus, in telling them that they do not really understand what they are requesting, asks them,

> Can you. . .be baptised with the baptism I am baptised with? *(10:38)*.

This clearly shows that Jesus considered baptism to be an immersion in the waters of suffering which was to be his passion and death.

Christians believe that both these themes of life and death, and salvation and suffering are present in the sacrament of baptism. Those who are baptised 'die with Christ' in suffering and also 'rise with Christ' in receiving eternal life. St Paul puts it like this:

'Have you forgotten that when we were baptised into union with Christ Jesus we were baptised into his death? By baptism we were buried with him, and lay dead, in order that, as Christ was raised from the dead in the splendour of the Father, so also we might set our feet upon the new path of life' (Romans 6:3–4).

These words of Paul go to the very heart of the meaning of baptism. The death he speaks of is the death to sin. Sin separates people from God. Christians believe that a person cannot really live if they are separated from God. Through baptism, they believe that a person is freed from sin and enters into a new life with God. Suffering and death give way to life with God which is salvation.

Baptism by the Holy Spirit
Mark says that Jesus came to baptise with the Holy Spirit. Christians believe that at baptism the Holy Spirit enters a person, gives new life, and claims that person now belongs to God. To receive the Holy Spirit in baptism is the same as saying that a person is now 'in Christ'. Just as two people who love each other grow more and more like each other and share the same life, so a person 'in Christ' grows more like him. This is made possible by the Holy Spirit.

The Christian believes that Jesus died and was raised from the dead so that anyone might be freed from sin and enter into a new life with God which is called 'life in the Spirit'. The sign of God's grace in giving this new life is the sacrament of baptism in water and the Holy Spirit.

The signs of the sacrament of baptism
When a person comes to be baptised the priest or minister will pour water over that person's head and will say special words. The words are 'I baptise you in the name of the Father, and of the Son, and of the Holy Spirit'. This originates from the command of Jesus to the Apostles where he commanded them to go into the whole world and 'baptise men everywhere in the name of the Father and of the Son and of the Holy Spirit' (Matthew 28:19). This is the main sacramental sign of baptism.

A second sign is that the person being baptised is marked with a cross, a further indication of suffering and death. This is to show that they now belong to Jesus. Christians believe that these signs are indelible: that is, they cannot be wiped away. This does not mean that the person automatically becomes a good Christian. Baptism is not a piece of magic or some sort of spiritual vaccination against evil. It means that the person now belongs to God.

Entry into the Church
Through baptism a person becomes a member of the Church. St Paul expresses this thought in his first letter to Corinth.

'For Christ is like a single body with its many limbs and organs, which, many as they are, together make up one body. For indeed we were all brought into one body by baptism, in the one Spirit, whether we are Jews or Greeks, whether slaves or free men, and that one Holy Spirit was poured out for all of us to drink' (1 Corinthians 12:13).

The body of Christ is another title for the Church. St Paul also indicates that baptism is for everyone. There is no distinction of nationality, income, intelligence or anything else. All people are equal in the sight of God. All can be members of the fellowship of the Church.

Infant baptism
The baptism of infants is by far the most common in the Christian Church today. It has been in use since very early times. The reason for infant baptism is the desire of the parents to bring up their children as Christians. As baptism is the sacrament of initiation, it seems natural to begin at this point. Some people, however, question how a baby can receive the sign of new life and faith. The answer is that it receives the sign in the same way as it receives everything for life; by depending on adults. The baby is not baptised because it believes but because there is a wish on the part of the parents to not only have the child received into the family of the Church but also to pass on the faith. The main Churches that baptise infants are the Roman Catholic, Greek Orthodox, Church of England and Methodist.

Adult baptism (believers' baptism)
In the early Church, people were baptised by immersion. They entered into a river or a pool and were submerged in its waters. They understood they were dying, because of their

sin, and were being buried in the waters in order to rise from the waters to a new life in Christ. The Baptist Church, for example, still administers baptism this way. It is called 'believers' baptism' and is only given to those old enough to make their own profession of faith in Jesus Christ.

Most other churches practise adult baptism for people who were not baptised as infants. This would normally be done after a period of instruction (called by some the 'catecumenate'). Obviously the adult is aware of the promises he or she is about to make and the meaning of baptism before receiving it. The main churches that prefer to baptise only adults are the Baptist, Christian Brethren and the Pentecostal.

The unity of baptism

The sacrament of baptism unites the majority of the Christian Churches. As long as the baptism is given under the sign of water and the Trinitarian words, as stated above, then it is accepted by most Christians as valid. This is most important. It acts as a solid foundation in the seeking of unity between all Christians.

Study Skills

Knowledge

1 What is a sacrament?
2 Where did John baptise people?
3 Give a summary of the preaching of John the Baptist.
4 What did John say was the difference between the baptism he offered and that which Jesus was to give?
5 What did the 'voice from heaven' say at the baptism of Jesus?
6 What words are used by the priest or minister at the moment of baptism?
7 How did St Paul describe the Church?
8 What is baptism by total immersion?

Understanding

9 Explain what difficulties are raised by the baptism of Jesus.
10 What do you understand to be the meaning of baptism for Christians today?

Evaluation

11 Why do you think Jesus chose to be baptised?
12 Give the reasons for and against the practice of infant baptism.

Which do you think is the stronger case? Why do you think this?

Practical Work

- Make arrangements to attend a baptismal service in your own local church. Note the various signs of the sacrament and try to discover what each sign means.

Different Names for the Eucharist

The eucharist is known by different names in different churches. Below are the main names by which it is known.

- **Eucharist**: this name comes from a Greek word meaning 'thanksgiving'. The emphasis is on the Church meeting to give thanks for the death and Resurrection of Jesus.
- **Holy Communion**: the word 'communion' means sharing as in a family. The emphasis is on the Church coming together as the family of God.
- **Lord's Supper**: this phrase was first used by St Paul (1 Corinthians 11:20). Jesus and the disciples shared the Last Supper together. The emphasis is on the Church sharing in that supper as his disciples.
- **Breaking of bread**: bread was broken and shared at the Last Supper. So the Church meets to do the same. The emphasis is on a simple meal that reminds Christians that Jesus gave himself on the Cross and rose again from the dead.
- **Mass**: used mainly in the Roman Catholic tradition, the word comes from the final sentence of the celebration which used to be said in Latin; 'ite, missa est' meaning 'go, you are dismissed'. The people are sent out into the community, having shared in the celebration of the sacrifice of Jesus.

The Eucharist Against the Background of Passover

Mark informs his readers that the Last Supper, which Jesus celebrated with his disciples, was the Jewish Feast of Passover. To understand what was happening at the Last Supper, it is important to set the meal against the background of the Passover.

The First Passover

The Passover meal commemorates the Exodus, the greatest
event in Jewish history. It tells how Moses was sent by God
to free the children of Israel from their captivity in Egypt.
After a long struggle with Pharaoh Moses finally succeeded in
taking the children of Israel away from Egypt and out into
the Sinai desert (Exodus 7:14–15:21).

In the narrow sense of the words, 'pass over' recalls the
time when the angel of death 'passed over' the houses of the
Israelites on their way to slay the first born of each Egyptian
family (Exodus 12:12). On that night Moses commanded the
Jews to sacrifice a lamb and smear the blood on the
doorposts of their house as a sign that they were to be
'passed over'. They were also to eat a meal consisting of roast
lamb, unleavened bread and bitter herbs (Exodus 12:8–11).
The Passover became a symbol for more than just the slaying
of the Egyptians' eldest sons. It very quickly became the
symbol of the whole 'passing over' from slavery to freedom
and it is this wider meaning that is celebrated each year as
the family meet for the Passover. This was the greatest night
of the year as the family feasted together and remembered
the Exodus.

The Passover Meal

The celebration of the Passover is divided into four main
sections.

1 *Introduction*
   (a) The meal begins with a blessing of the first cup by the
       eldest male present (i.e. Paterfamilias). This cup is
       drunk as a symbol of joy at being able to celebrate the
       Passover.
   (b) With the first cup of wine, a dish of bitter herbs and a
       purée of such fruits as figs, dates and almonds is
       served. Not only is this dish to stimulate the appetite
       but is also to remind them of their bitter captivity in
       Egypt.
   (c) The main meal is then served but not yet eaten. The
       second cup of wine is poured but not drunk.

2 *The Passover liturgy*
   (a) The story of the Passover is told by the Paterfamilias
       in response to the question of the youngest member of

the family: 'What is the meaning of this night?'

(b) This free outline of the story of the first Passover, which is called the 'Haggadah', is responded to with the singing of the first part of the special Passover Psalms, which are called the 'Hallel Psalms' (Psalms 112–113).

(c) This is followed by the drinking of the second cup of wine called the 'Hallel cup'.

3   *The Passover meal*

(a) The main meal begins with words of blessing over the unleavened bread, which symbolises the urgency of the first Passover (Exodus 12:11). The words of blessing would most probably be:

'Praise to you, Lord, King of the universe who causes bread to come from the earth.'

(b) The eating of the lamb, bread and the rest of the bitter herbs follows.

(c) The meal ends with the blessing and drinking of the third cup. Again the words of blessing would probably be:

'Praise to you, Lord, King of the universe who feeds the world with goodness. . .'.

This cup is passed round as a celebration of all the goodness of God shown to his people.

4   *Conclusion*

(a) The meal finishes with the singing of the second part of the Hallel Psalms (Psalm 114–118).

(b) After this joyous celebration, the final act is the sharing of the fourth and last cup of wine.

The Account of the Last Supper in Mark (14:22–25)

Jesus met with the twelve for the Passover meal. It was a family meal and for the Jews the meal time was not just a question of satisfying hunger. For the Jew, sitting at table with others for food indicated a desire to offer peace and friendship. This Passover meal, celebrating the event of the Exodus was the most important meal in the Jewish year. Three different things happened at the Last Supper as recorded by Mark.

(a) **The warning about Judas**. The first thing Jesus did, at the
Last Supper, was to give a warning about the one who was
to betray him. He was one of the twelve who was present at
the table. There is no evidence that the other disciples
suspected Judas. Perhaps Jesus was making a last appeal to
Judas before it was too late.

(b) **The words of institution**. During the supper Jesus said
some words over the bread and wine. These words are
known as the words of institution (this means the words
spoken by Jesus over the bread and wine when he celebrated
this meal for the first time).

> Take this: this is my body. . .This is my blood, the
> blood of the covenant, shed for many (14:22–24).

'*This is my body*': in using this phrase Jesus speaks of himself
as the broken bread which is the fate of his own body. This
is given in sacrifice.

'*This my blood, the blood of the covenant, shed for many*': Mark,
again, uses the wine to symbolise his blood which will be
given in sacrifice for all.

Jesus refers to the covenant in his words over the cup. The
covenant is the name given to the agreement between God
and humanity. The chief figure in Israel's history of the
covenant was Moses and it was he, who having received the
terms of the covenant in the form of the Ten Commandments,
sprinkled blood on the people as a sign of their faithfulness.
In referring to the covenant in the sense of his blood, Jesus is
now making the final covenant. Christians believe that
through Jesus, men and women can draw near to God, know
God, and experience God.

In sharing out the bread and wine in this way, Jesus was
showing the disciples that his body would be broken and his
blood would be shed just like the bread which he had
broken and passed round and the wine which had been
poured out at the table.

(c) **The vow of abstinence**.

> . . . never again shall I drink from the fruit of the vine
> until the day when I drink it new in the kingdom of
> God (14:25).

These words are normally taken to mean that Jesus is saying

he is going to die. This will be the last time he will pass such a cup round at any meal.

There is, however, a second meaning that can be given to the words. Jesus is saying that not only is the end near but that he is about to complete his work. His life now belongs to God and his coming kingdom. The kingdom of God will only be completed at the end of time (see chapter 10). This reflects the Jewish idea of the Messianic banquet. Jesus will celebrate with his followers once again at the end of time.

The meaning of the Eucharist for Christians today

The two traditions of the Eucharist

There are four accounts of the words of institution in the New Testament. It is obvious, however, that these come from two different traditions. Paul and Luke follow one tradition which is probably the earliest; Mark and Matthew follow the other. A comparison of the accounts shows the great similarity of thought between them.

1   The account of Paul and Luke
(*Words in italics* – found only in Paul. **Words in bold** – found only in Luke.)

'This is my body, which is for you; do this as a memorial of me.'
'This cup, **poured out for you**, is the new covenant sealed by my blood.
Whenever you drink it, do this as a memorial of me' (1 Corinthians 11:24–25; Luke 22:19–20).

2   The accounts of Mark and Matthew
(*Words in italics* – found only in Mark. **Words in bold** – found only in Matthew.)

'Take this; **(and eat)** this is my body.'
"**Drink from it all of you.** This is my blood, the blood of the covenant, shed for many **for the forgiveness of sins**. I tell you *this*: never again shall I drink from the fruit of the vine until that day when I drink it new **with you** in the kingdom *of God* **(of my Father)**' (Mark 14:22–25; Matthew 26:26–29).

Disagreement

Unfortunately, the Christian Churches disagree about the meaning and practice of the eucharist. This is one of the main obstacles to Church unity. The very act which should have been the unifying factor within Christianity – the celebration of the eucharist – became a matter of disunity.

The problem lies in:

1   *the interpretation of the words of Jesus;*
2   *the interpretation of what happens to the bread and wine; and*
3   *the meaning of the service by whatever name it is called.*

The main historical differences are:

(a) **Roman Catholic and Eastern Orthodox traditions**.
Christians of these two traditions believe that the bread and wine used in the eucharist actually become the body and blood of Jesus.

The whole celebration is one of sacrifice based on Jesus' words. The body and blood of Jesus are offered as sacrifice but this does not mean that Jesus is being sacrificed afresh every time the Mass is celebrated. When the Church celebrates Mass it is not offering a new sacrifice. There was only one sacrifice and that was the death of Jesus on the Cross. What it does mean is that the one and only sacrifice of Jesus is made present. It is re-presented in the bread and the wine of the Mass. The words 'Do this as a memorial of me' are not interpreted as simply meaning 'in memory of'. The words are interpreted in the sense of 'doing it' as though it were the first time.

When the people receive the bread and wine they believe that they are really receiving the body and blood of Jesus.

(b) **The Protestant tradition**. *The Protestant interpretation of the eucharist can be summed up by examining the ideas of three of the well known protestant reformers of the sixteenth century.*

(i) Martin Luther. *The view of the Eucharist based on the ideas of Martin Luther is that Jesus is really present in, with, and beneath the bread and wine offered in the celebration. This does not, however, mean that there is any real change in the substance of the bread and wine. Not many Christians, outside of the Lutheran Church hold this view although some of the Anglo-Catholics of the Church of England hold to views that are similar to both this and that of the Roman Catholic tradition.*

(ii) John Calvin. *This view is that Jesus is really present in the bread and wine of the eucharist, as it is consumed, in a spiritual way.*

There is no suggestion of any change in the substance of the bread and wine and after the eucharist is over that which is left remains bread and wine. The spiritual presence of Jesus is only present as the elements are eaten and drunk.

Originally the Anglican reformers of the sixteenth century shared Calvin's view. So did the Non-Conformists, especially the Methodists. Today this view is still held by the broad stream of the Church of England although most of the Non-Conformist Churches have slowly turned away to a third view.

(iii) Ulrich Zwingli. *Zwingli was a Swiss reformer. The view that is attributed to his name is that the bread and wine used at the eucharist are only symbols. They are used merely as symbols of remembrance or memorial. This is the view held by most Free Churches and the Evangelical wing of the Church of England.*

Agreement

Most Christians are agreed that it is important to bring about an end to this disunity as soon as possible. Therefore, to consider the eucharist, not in terms of where there is disagreement but in terms of where there is agreement is the positive way forward.

There is some agreement and this is of great value. The vast majority of Christian Churches are agreed on the central part which the eucharist plays in their faith. They accept, without question, the following points about the eucharist.

1   *Jesus instituted the meal at the Last Supper.*
2   *When the Church meets to celebrate the eucharist Jesus is present in the whole celebration and is received by faith.*
3   *The eucharist calls to mind the death and resurrection of Jesus.*
4   *The celebrating of the eucharist is a means of communion with Jesus and each other.*
5   *Through the eucharist, the Church looks forward to the time when Jesus will come again and establish the kingdom of God on earth.*

Many Christians believe that it is from this common ground that the churches must begin to look for ways of coming together to share their faith. Their hope is that one day all Christians will be able to celebrate the eucharist together, at the same table, during the same meal and in communion, as they break bread together.

Study Skills

Knowledge

1 Give three other names for the eucharist.
2 Why did the Jews celebrate the Passover?
3 What was eaten at the Passover?
4 Who was the Paterfamilias?
5 What is the Haggadah?
6 What words did Jesus say over the wine at the Last Supper?
7 What does the word 'covenant' mean?

Understanding

8 What do you understand Jesus to mean by the words he says over the bread and wine at the Last Supper?
9 What do you understand to be the main differences in the interpretation of the eucharist amongst the Christian Churches today?

Evaluation

10 What do you think the words Jesus said at the Last Supper mean for Christians today?
11 How important do you think the eucharist is for Christians today? Why do you think the Churches hold differing views of the meaning of this sacrament?

Examination Practice

Describe the baptism of Jesus by John the Baptist as recorded in Mark's Gospel.   (4)
Explain the meaning of the words spoken by the voice of God at the baptism of Jesus.   (4)
Name three things Christians, today, believe about the sacrament of baptism.   (3)
Describe what happened at the Last Supper as stated in Mark's Gospel.   (4)
How do Christians differ in their views of the meaning of Jesus' words spoken over the bread and wine?   (5)

Practical Work

● Invite representatives of the different churches to give a short talk and answer questions about their own church's interpretation of the eucharist. Try to establish what common ground there is between the churches.

8 The Suffering and Death of Jesus

The suffering and death of Jesus is such an important part of Mark's Gospel that considerable time must be given to its study. There are four areas of study to be covered:

- The narrative of the last week of Jesus.
- The emphasis on suffering and death in the Gospel.
- 'Why did Jesus die?'
- What does the death of Jesus mean for Christians today?

The Narrative of the Last Week of Jesus

Mark has arranged the events of the last days of Jesus into one week. This is, in all probability, a condensed reconstruction as the events in Jerusalem may well have taken longer than a single week.

Scholars believe the Passion narrative was the earliest continuous account of events in the life of Jesus to take a fixed form. It may be that Mark made the events fit into a single week because the early Church was already celebrating a 'holy week' and therefore, one week gave a structure to their early Christian celebrations. The events of the last week can be tabulated, remembering that the Jewish day begins at 6.00 pm.

SUNDAY (6.00 pm Sat – 6.00 pm Sun)

The Entry into Jerusalem 11:1–11

MONDAY (6.00 pm Sun – 6.00 pm Mon)

The cursing of the fig tree 11:12–14
The cleansing of the Temple 11:15–19

TUESDAY (6.00 pm Mon – 6.00 pm Tues)

The question of authority 11:27–33
The parable of the tenants 12:1–12

Sunday (6.00 pm Sat – 6.00 pm Sun)

The Entry into Jerusalem (11:1–11)
The claim of Jesus to be the Messiah is made public as he rode into Jerusalem on a donkey. This emphasised the fact that he was a peaceful Messiah and not a military leader. Even though Mark does not quote the Old Testament source of this story, there is no doubt that the Messianic verse of the prophet Zechariah stands behind this account:

'. . .see, your King is coming to you,
his cause won, his victory gained,
humble and mounted on an ass,
on a foal, the young of a she-ass' (Zechariah 9:9).

Mark prefers to quote Psalm 118:25–26:

Blessings on him who comes in the name of the Lord *(11:10)*.

He sees the Messiahship of Jesus in

. . .the coming kingdom of our father David *(11:10)*.

These words emphasise the role of Jesus as Messiah. Mark could be telling his readers that the crowd recognised Jesus as Messiah, but during the course of the week came to think of him as a 'fraud' and were calling for his death by the end of the week. The words of the Psalm, however, were used also to call down a blessing on pilgrims entering Jerusalem for the festival of Passover. Therefore, it is not clear whether ordinary people would have seen any real meaning in the action of Jesus.

Some scholars have suggested that Jesus rode into Jerusalem at the time of the Feast of Dedication. This feast celebrated the dedication of the Temple and as part of the celebration branches were waved and Psalm 118 chanted. It may be that the onlookers did not see any Messianic meaning in Jesus' actions.

Christians, however, have an annual celebration of Jesus' triumphant entry into Jerusalem as Messiah on Palm Sunday, the Sunday before Easter.

Monday (6.00 pm Sun – 6.00 pm Mon)

The Cursing of the Fig Tree (11:12–14)
This is a difficult incident to understand for the action of

Jesus seems out of character. Mark himself states that it would have been remarkable for Jesus to have found any fruit for it was not even the season for figs. It has been suggested that the story was originally a parable (see Luke 13:6–9), aimed at the Pharisees, which is now out of context. Mark has treated the story as an actual event. The most likely explanation is that the fig tree stood for the self-righteous, people like the Pharisees, who made a great show of their religion but produced few results. They are condemned. Soon it would be too late and Jerusalem, the centre of this religion would be destroyed.

The Cleansing of the Temple (11:15–19)

In the prophecy of Malachi it says, 'suddenly the Lord whom you seek will come to his Temple' (Malachi 3:1). It may be that this prophecy lies behind the account of the expulsion from the Temple of those who bought and sold.

According to Mark Jesus entered the Temple and:

1 drove out those who bought and sold;
2 upset the tables of the money changers;
3 upset the chairs of those who sold the sacrificial pigeons; and
4 stopped people carrying things through the Temple, using it as a short cut.

Traders in the Temple sold sacrifices to pilgrims coming to Jerusalem. These sacrifices had to be bought with Temple money because foreign currency such as Roman coins showed the heads of pagan rulers or gods. This was against the Jewish law. In addition, the suggestion has been made that the rates of exchange favoured the Temple. The profits of all this trading went to the priests. This corruption was hated by the ordinary Jew. Using the Temple as a short cut was forbidden by the law. Yet the priests allowed it.

Jesus in challenging this use of the Temple also challenged the authority of the chief priests. The words of Jesus are a combination of Isaiah (56:7) and Jeremiah (7:11)

'My house shall be called a house of prayer for all the nations'. But you have made it a robbers' cave (11:17).

It is surprising that Jesus could get away with such action. Mark records that the chief priests and Scribes looked for some way of getting rid of Jesus but used the excuse that he was, at this time, popular with the people.

Tuesday (6.00 pm Mon – 6.00 pm Tues)

- The question of authority (see chapter 6).
- The Parable of the Wicked Husbandmen (see chapter 3).
- The question about taxes to Caesar (see chapter 6).
- The question about resurrection (see chapter 6).
- The question about the greatest Commandment (see chapter 6).

Wednesday (6.00 pm Tues – 6.00 pm Wed)

The Plot Against Jesus (14:1–2)
The story of the Passion continues with the statement by the chief priests and Scribes that they were seeking to arrest Jesus and put him to death. They decided, however, that they could not do this during the coming festival of Passover because the people still followed Jesus and they did not want unrest among the people. It is possible to pinpoint this decision of the chief priests and Scribes. Mark records

> . . .the Festival of Passover and Unleavened Bread was only two days off *(14:1)*.

FESTIVAL OF UNLEAVENED BREAD

- Originally this was a separate feast to Passover.
- By the time of Jesus the two festivals were celebrated at the same time.
- Leaven was a substance used to make bread rise.
- It was a piece of dough kept back from the previous baking.
- The main symbol of the feast was the use of *unleavened* bread for a whole week.
- This was to symbolise a break with the past and all its sin and the making of a fresh start.

The Anointing at Bethany (14:3–9)
The anointing of Jesus takes place in the house of Simon the leper, in Bethany. Tradition claims that the woman

responsible is Mary of Magdala although there is no evidence for this at all. Although Mark does not name the woman, in John's Gospel, she is named as Mary, the sister of Martha and Lazarus.

The story is symbolic:

1 kings were anointed at their crowning;
2 priests were anointed on taking office;
3 bodies were anointed after death for burial. Jesus claims that the woman anointed him in readiness for death; and
4 the 'Messiah' means 'anointed one'.

Therefore, Mark is using this story to show that Jesus, as Messiah, was about to suffer and die.

Judas Plans his Betrayal (14:10–11)

Judas decided to betray Jesus and told the chief priests that he would lead them to Jesus so that they could arrest him secretly. This would avoid causing trouble with the people (14:2).

Various suggestions have been made as to why Judas betrayed Jesus.

1 Matthew makes him out to be a greedy man who wanted money. Yet Mark makes it clear that money was not the main motive. Anyway, the amount of money involved was not very large. (In Matthew's Gospel the sum of thirty pieces of silver is mentioned which was the price of a slave.)
2 In both Luke and John's Gospels there is a claim that Satan entered Judas. John goes further and not only calls Judas a thief but also says that he was chosen by God to perform the evil deed.
3 It has been suggested that the real reason Judas betrayed Jesus was because he wanted Jesus to be the popular Messiah of the day who would drive out the Romans. He either tried to force Jesus' hand to make him fight or he had become disappointed in him and acted out of bitterness.

What does the betrayal of Judas really mean? There are two views. The first is the most popular. The betrayal was leading the Temple police to Jesus. After all, before Jesus could be arrested he must be found. Judas knew where he would be. Even though Jesus had moved freely among the crowds during the day, he had retired to Bethany each night except

the night he was arrested. Even the arrangements for the
Passover meal were done in secret. Therefore, the authorities
needed someone to lead them to where Jesus could be
arrested quietly. The second view is that Judas told the chief
priests that Jesus claimed to be some sort of Messiah;
perhaps one who would lead a rebellion against the Romans.
This is possible as it is obvious in Mark's gospel, that the
disciples did not really understand what the Messiahship of
Jesus meant.

Thursday (6.00 pm Wed – 6.00 pm Thurs)

Preparation for the Passover (14:12–16)
Mark makes it clear which day it is. It is Thursday. The
disciples are sent, by pre-arranged plan, to prepare a room in
Jerusalem for that evening's celebration of the Passover meal.
By tradition, the upper room was in the house of the mother
of John Mark, the author of the Gospel. There is no real
evidence for this other than the fact that in the Acts of the
Apostles, the house of John Mark's mother is known to be
the meeting-place of the disciples (Acts 12:12).

Mark also makes it clear that the preparations were for a
Passover meal. There is considerable dispute, however, as to
whether the Last Supper was a Passover meal. It has been
argued that Jesus could not have been executed on the Feast
day of the Passover because:

1 the priests would not have held a trial on a feast day; and
2 execution on a feast day was impossible according to
   Jewish law.

Scholars holding this view direct attention to three further
pieces of information to support it:

1 the food usually eaten at Passover (e.g. lamb; bitter herbs;
   unleavened bread) is not mentioned;
2 the special words used at the Passover (called the
   Haggadah) are not mentioned; and
3 John's Gospel claims that the Passover that year was on
   the Sabbath (6.00 pm Fri – 6.00 pm Sat). Jesus was dead
   before the Passover day began and therefore the Last
   Supper could not have been the Passover meal.

This is a difficult problem. But there is a simple solution. At
that time there was a dispute between the Pharisees and

Sadducees as to when the festival should begin. The Pharisees were allowed to hold the meal one day before the official date. Jesus could have been following the custom of the Pharisees by celebrating Passover on the Thursday evening.

There is no doubt that Mark intends his readers to understand the meal as that of the Passover. There are striking similarities between what Mark tells us happened at the Last Supper and the Passover meal:

1   there was a dish (could this refer to the bitter herbs?) (14:20);
2   there were words spoken over the bread and wine; this followed the pattern of the Passover when the head of the family (called the Paterfamilias) had to explain the significance of the food and drink (14:22–25);
3   the bread was blessed and broken during the meal. This was rare in Jewish custom; it was demanded at the Passover meal (14:22);
4   red wine was used; this was another regulation of the Passover liturgy (14:24); and
5   hymns (psalms) were sung after the meal. This was another regulation of the Passover liturgy (14:26).

(For a fuller discussion of the Passover, see chapter 7)

Friday (6.00 pm Thurs – 6.00 pm Fri)

The Last Supper
Mark states that the meal was eaten during the evening, the beginning of Passover day (6.00 pm).

(a) **The treachery of Judas foretold** (14:17–21) (see notes on 14:10–11).

(b) **The institution of the eucharist** (14:22–25). These verses are very important to Christians. They are central to the celebration of the Christian eucharist.

> . . .this is my body. . .This is my blood, the blood of the Covenant, shed for many.

This is the language of sacrifice. The breaking of bread and the pouring of wine symbolised the death of Jesus. Christians believe that through the death of Jesus a new relationship is made between God and his people. This relationship is called the 'Covenant'. As the Jews at Passover remembered the

Exodus, the time of God's deliverance of his people from their slavery in Egypt, so Christians see in the Eucharist God's deliverance of his people from sin. A new relationship with God is possible through the death and resurrection of Jesus.

(c) **Peter's denial foretold** (14:26–31). After singing the Passover psalms, Jesus and his disciples went out to the Mount of Olives. On Passover night no one was allowed to leave the city, so Jesus could not return to Bethany as he had done on previous nights that week. However, because of the massive numbers in Jerusalem at Passover time, the regulations were relaxed to allow the pilgrims to spend the night in a larger area just outside the city. The Mount of Olives was within that allowed area. As they were on their way to a small garden called Gethsemane on the Mount of Olives Jesus told his disciples that they would desert him.

Peter said he would never lose faith. Jesus forecast that before the cock crowed twice Peter would have denied any relationship with Jesus three times. It was forbidden to keep cockerels within the city of Jerusalem so in all probability the 'cock crow' was an early morning 'watch' of the Roman day, perhaps a trumpet call.

The Garden of Gethsemane (14:32–42)
Jesus took Peter, James and John into the garden, the rest of the disciples having been told to wait for them. Peter, James and John were told to pray while Jesus went further into the garden to pray by himself. Three times he returned and found the three asleep. The humanity of Jesus is seen in this story.

> Abba, Father. . .all things are possible to thee; take this cup away from me. Yet not what I will, but what thou wilt *(14:36).*

This prayer expresses the closest relationship between God and Jesus. Jesus was aware that suffering (the cup) lay ahead and he was frightened. He prayed to be released but only if it was God's will. The story ends with the coming of Judas. The hour had come. Betrayal loomed.

The Arrest of Jesus (14:43–52)
Judas had arranged a signal with the men sent by the chief priests, Scribes and elders. The signal was one of great simplicity, a kiss. This was the common form of greeting.

Judas came up to Jesus and kissed him. Jesus was arrested and in the struggle that followed the high priest's servant was injured.

Jesus accepted his lot because he said it was in keeping with the scriptures. He did not say which scriptures but there are several passages from the Old Testament that speak of the act of betrayal played out in the garden of Gethsemane.

For example:

'All who hate me whisper together about me,
and love to make the worst of everything. . .
Even the friend whom I trusted,
who ate at my table,
exults over my misfortune.' (Psalm 41:7 and 9).

The final comment on the disciples is made by Mark.

> Then the disciples all deserted him and ran
> away *(14:50)*.

The disciples do not reappear in the Gospel story. They disappear in failure and desertion.

At this point Mark records the strange story of the young man who was also seized but who slipped out of his 'linen cloth' and escaped naked. It has been suggested that the young man was Mark himself. This would make sense especially if the house where the Last Supper took place was in fact the house belonging to Mark's mother.

The Trial Before the Sanhedrin (14:53–65)
The Sanhedrin is the official court of Jewish justice (see chapter 1).

If Jesus was on trial then there are certain irregularities in the proceedings as recorded by Mark:

1   the Sanhedrin did not usually meet at the high priest's house (14:53);
2   trials which involved the possible sentence of death were not allowed at night (14:55);
3   a verdict of guilty required that the sentence should be delayed for twenty-four hours;
4   witnesses were warned that if they gave false evidence they would suffer the same verdict which would have been awarded to the accused (14:56–57);

5   at least two independent witnesses had to agree on their evidence; if witnesses disagreed the trial was stopped and a 'not guilty' verdict was pronounced (14:59); and
6   it was a mockery of the legal system to allow the beating of a prisoner during the court proceedings (14:65).

It may well be that this was not a trial but more of an interrogation to see if a case could be made for taking Jesus to the Roman Governor.

Throughout the trial Jesus remained silent, as the false evidence was given by witnesses who could not agree with each other. It was only when asked the direct question by the high priest,

> Are you the Messiah, the Son of the Blessed One?

that Jesus spoke,

> Jesus said, 'I am' *(14:62)*.

This was enough to seal Jesus' fate. Now he could be taken to Pontius Pilate, the Roman Governor with a recommendation that he suffer the death penalty. The high priest, in tearing his clothes, declared that a formal act of blasphemy had been committed.

The Denial of Peter (14:66–72)
Peter is accused three times, as he sits in the courtyard of the high priest's house, of being one of Jesus' men and three times he denies it. He had probably been seen with Jesus in and around Jerusalem. Twice the servant girl accuses him, the third time a general accusation is made on the grounds of Peter's strong northern accent. Peter, cursing and swearing, denies his knowledge of Jesus. The cock crew and Peter bursts into tears.

The Trial Before Pilate (15:1–15)
Pontius Pilate was the Governor of Judea from 26 to 36 AD. The picture of him presented by the New Testament is much kinder than history remembers him. All the Gospels portray Pilate as a man who was reluctant to condemn Jesus and who would have preferred to set him free. This is understandable when one realises that the Gospels were written at a time when the Church had to exist in a Roman world. It was also the intention of the evangelists to blame the Jews as directly responsible for the death of Jesus.

The charge brought to Pilate was that Jesus claimed to be

'the King of the Jews' (see chapter 2). Certainly if Jesus were guilty of this charge then it was a threat to the Romans, however small. Pilate did not consider Jesus to be such a threat and tried to have him released.

He offered to set Jesus free instead of Barabbas. There is no historical evidence for the custom of releasing a prisoner at festival time although such an amnesty was possible. Barabbas was a nationalist who had led some minor revolt against the Romans and was, therefore, something of a local hero. The crowd shouted for the release of Barabbas and the death of Jesus. Pilate declared that Jesus had done no wrong but in the end, in order to pacify the mob, he agreed to the crucifixion of Jesus. Life was cheap.

The apparent dilemma for Pilate is that he considered Jesus to be innocent and did not want to condemn an innocent man. He did not want to give in to the Jews. Why then did Pilate give in to the Jews?

Pilate's crime was one of weakness. The most probable reason is that he was afraid of a riot breaking out in the crowded capital during the festival. Such trouble might well have resulted in a recall to Rome. Such an event had happened by the time the Gospel was written.

The Mockery of Jesus (15:16–20)
It is usually thought that scourging was the normal practice before crucifixion by the Romans. There seems, however, little evidence for this from historical records. Crucifixion was meant to be a slow and painful death and the flogging of the victim would have made death quicker. The scourging Jesus received may relate to the comment in the prophet Isaiah, '. . .by his scourging we are healed' (Isaiah 53:5). When the Romans flogged a prisoner they did so using a leather whip with metal or bone studs in the thongs. After the scourging the soldiers mocked Jesus by dressing him up in purple, the royal colour, and giving him a crown of thorns and a reed for a sceptre.

The Crucifixion
(a) **The Way of the Cross** (15:21–22). Mark records that Simon of Cyrene was forced into carrying the cross for Jesus. Simon had two sons, Alexander and Rufus, who were to become members of the Church (Romans 16:13). The fact that Mark makes no attempt to explain who Alexander and Rufus were must mean that his audience knew who they were. Perhaps they belonged to the Christian Church in Rome.

The Crucifixion took place at Golgotha (Hebrew), the place of the skull (Calvary in Greek).

(b) **The Crucifixion** (15:23–29). On arrival at Golgotha, Jesus was offered 'wine mixed with myrrh'. This was a drug that would help to ease the acute pain that crucifixion brought to the victim. Jesus refused it.

Mark tells us that the soldiers divided Jesus' clothing casting lots to see what each would get. This may well be a piece of writing based on Psalm 21:18.

Jesus was crucified, nailed to the cross beam by his wrists before it was hoisted up and fixed to the permanent upright of the cross. His feet were also nailed. The body was supported by a small block of wood at the bottom of the spine. Crucifixion was a slow death by suffocation, the prisoner alternating between pushing himself upright in order to breathe and sagging back to rest and relieve the pain.

It was nine in the morning when the Crucifixion took place. The name of the criminal was normally fixed on the cross. In the case of Jesus it said 'the King of the Jews'. It was common practice to state the crime of the victim. Jesus did not die alone. Two bandits were executed with him.

(c) **The crucified Jesus is mocked** (15:29–32). Jesus was mocked by: those passing by; the chief priests and scribes; and the two criminals crucified with him. The mockery consisted of two taunts:

1   that Jesus had claimed to destroy the temple and rebuild it in three days. If he could do this then surely he could come down from the cross and save himself; and
2   if he was the Christ, the King of Israel, then let him come down from the cross and convince people.

(d) **The death of Jesus** (15:33–39). The account of the death of Jesus in Mark's Gospel begins with the comment about 'darkness' being over the 'whole land' from the sixth hour (12 noon) until the ninth hour (3.00 pm). Various suggestions have been made about the meaning of this darkness. It has been suggested that an eclipse of the sun took place.

Another suggestion is that it was a fulfillment of a prophecy such as, 'I will make the sun go down at noon and darken the earth in broad daylight' (Amos 8:9).

Perhaps the best interpretation is that Mark is trying to

show his readers the importance of this event; the extreme suffering and death of Jesus which is the major theme of the Gospel.

The only words Jesus spoke from the cross in Mark are in Aramaic:

> Eli, eli, lema sabachthani?
> My God, my God, Why hast thou forsaken
> me? *(15:34)*.

This is a quotation from Psalm 22:1. Some people find it hard to accept that Jesus would utter a cry of despair or feel deserted by God. They point to the triumphant end of the Psalm and claim that Jesus began to recite the Psalm but died before he could finish it. Others find it easy to accept that Jesus felt totally desolate and deserted by God. He was a man and died a human death in extreme pain and agony.

The crowd misunderstood the words of Jesus as a cry of help to the prophet Elijah. They offered him drugged wine to drink but it was too late. With a loud cry, Jesus died. Mark records that the curtain of the Temple; which covered the entrance to the Holy of Holies was torn in two from top to bottom. The Jews believed the Holy of Holies was the place where God was to be found. This tearing of the Temple curtain symbolised that the God who was hidden is now revealed to all people. The old religion of the Jews is now replaced.

Mark's moving story closes with the words of the centurion,

> Truly this man was the Son of God *(15:39)*.

The death of Jesus ends where the Gospel began with a clear statement that Jesus is the Son of God (15:39; 1:1) (see chapter 2).

(e) **The women watch at the Crucifixion** (15:40–41). Jesus died alone. The disciples were absent. They had failed. They had run away (14:50). At this point Mark introduces into the story the women who take over the role of the disciples. They were to fail as well (16:8). The women watched the crucifixion. Among them were Mary of Magdala, Mary the mother of James the younger and Joseph, and Salome (15:40).

The Burial (15:42–47)
It was now evening, says Mark, and the burial had to be

completed by 6.00 pm for then the Sabbath began and it was forbidden to bury on the Sabbath. They buried the dead outside the city in tombs cut out of rock, or in caves.

Joseph of Arimathaea, a member of the Sanhedrin, who was obviously sympathetic to Jesus, went to Pontius Pilate and asked for the body of Jesus. Joseph

...looked forward to the kingdom of God (15:43).

This means that Joseph longed for the coming of the Messiah. Pilate checked that Jesus was dead and gave his permission. Jesus was taken by Joseph and laid to rest in the tomb. The women took note of where the body of Jesus had been placed, intending to come back, after the Sabbath was over, to complete the burial arrangements.

This story emphasises two important points:

1 Jesus was really dead; and
2 it was certain where he had been buried.

This was important to the early Christians because two of the early charges the Christian Church had to face were that Jesus did not really die and that the women went to the wrong tomb on the Sunday morning.

Study Skills

Knowledge

1 What instructions did Jesus give when he sent the disciples to fetch the colt?
2 How did the Jewish leaders react to the cleansing of the Temple?
3 What instructions did Jesus give for the preparation of the Passover?
4 What happened in the garden of Gethsemane?
5 What did the false witnesses accuse Jesus of saying?
6 What did the high priest ask Jesus?
7 What was Jesus' reply?
8 Why did Jesus deserve to die according to Jewish law?
9 Who was the Roman Governor at this time?
10 Who carried Jesus' cross?
11 What does 'Golgotha' mean?
12 What happened to Jesus' clothes?
13 Who watched the Crucifixion?
14 Who asked for the body of Jesus and buried it in the tomb?

Understanding

15 What do you think the story of Jesus' entry into Jerusalem means?
16 Why did the Jewish leaders decide to get rid of Jesus after he had driven out those who bought and sold in the Temple?
17 Do you think the Last Supper was a Passover meal? Give reasons for your answer.

Evaluation

18 'If Jesus had not been crucified there would have been no Christianity.' Do you agree with this statement? Give reasons for your answer.

Practical Work

● Design and complete a wall chart showing the last week of Jesus' life as Mark records it. Include an inset showing the ground plan of Jerusalem at that time.

The Emphasis on Suffering and Death in the Gospel

This is the major theme of Mark's Gospel. The importance and necessity of suffering runs through the whole Gospel. There are many passages which must be examined in order to understand the importance Mark places on this theme.

The Baptism (1:1–11)

> Thou art my Son, My Beloved; on thee my favour rests *(1:11)*.

These words, spoken by God, at the baptism of Jesus are a combination of two Old Testament texts. 'You are my son. . .' comes from the Messianic Psalm 2 and 'on thee my favour rests' from the 'Suffering Servant Songs' of Isaiah (Isaiah 42:1) (see chapter 7). This was an announcement, even before the ministry of Jesus had begun, of a Messiah who would suffer.

A Discussion on Fasting (2:18–20)

> But the time will come when the bridegroom will be taken away from them *(2:20)*.

Mark intends his readers to see Jesus as the bridegroom. The words of Jesus tell of a time when the bridegroom will no longer be present. This is a reference to the death of Jesus. It is the earliest reference to Jesus' death in the Gospel.

The Man with the Withered Hand (3:1–6)

> But the Pharisees. . .began plotting against him with the partisans of Herod to see how they could make away with him *(3:6)*.

Mark is talking about the rejection of Jesus by the Jews. It appears very early in the Gospel. Mark uses the statement to show how Jesus will have to face death.

A Visit to Nazareth (6:1–6)

This paragraph stands for the rejection of Jesus by his own family and country. Finally, this rejection will be by the whole of Israel as the story of Jesus ends in death by Crucifixion.

The Passion Predictions (8:31; 9:31; 10:33–34)

> And he began to teach them that the Son of Man had to undergo great sufferings, and to be rejected by the elders, chief priests, and doctors of the law; to be put to death, and to rise again three days afterwards *(8:31)*.

> The Son of Man is now to be given up into the power of men, and they will kill him, and three days after being killed, he will rise again *(9:31)*.

> We are now going up to Jerusalem. . .and the Son of Man will be given up to the chief priests and the doctors of the law; they will condemn him to death and hand him over to the foreign power. He will be mocked and spat upon, flogged and killed; and three days afterwards, he will rise again *(10:33–34)*.

There are two ways to look at the Passion predictions.

1　The Passion predictions are Jesus' words in the sense of prophecy.
2　The Passion predictions are a construction by Mark based on his Passion narrative and are meant to emphasise the suffering and death of Jesus.

A lot of scholars favour the latter alternative. They believe the Passion narrative was written first. Then Mark based the predictions of suffering and death on that narrative.

The Sons of Zebedee (10:35–40)

This passage is difficult. Throughout the Passion predictions no-one in Mark's Gospel seems to understand the meaning of the suffering that is going to happen. Yet in this story James and John ask a question which seems to show either a deep understanding of Messiahship or that they were thinking of Jesus' Messiahship in political terms.

> Grant us the right to sit in state with you, one at your right and the other at your left (10:37).

The reply of Jesus continues the theme of suffering. The 'baptism' and 'cup' are symbols of suffering. Jesus is saying that all he can promise is his own experience of suffering, an experience to come.

The Parable of the Wicked Husbandmen (12:1–12)

Whatever the original meaning of the parable, Mark uses it in its allegorical form. The parable based on Isaiah 5:1–7 has well known allegorical features (see chapter 3). The most important is the identification of Jesus with the son. The son is rejected and killed.

The Anointing at Bethany (14:3–9)

This story comes just before the Passion narrative. The interest focuses on verse 8.

> She has done what lay in her power; she is beforehand with anointing my body for burial.

This means that Jesus received the funeral rites in advance. Mark concludes that Jesus expected to die in the near future.

The Institution of the Eucharist (14:22–25)

The summary of Jesus' words of interpretation over the bread and wine are:

Take: this is my body.
This (wine) is my blood of the covenant poured out for many.

The words speak of sacrifice. At the Last Supper, Jesus as 'Paterfamilias' gives a new interpretation to the Passover. He identifies both the bread and wine with himself, given as a sacrificial offering. The bread is compared to his body, surrendered in death. The wine is the blood of the covenant. The sacrifice shortly to be made on the cross is the shedding of blood that will bring into being God's covenant relationship with all people.

The Garden of Gethsemane (14:32–42)

The story of the agony in the garden of Gethsemane is the most descriptive in the synoptic Gospels. Jesus told his disciples that his heart was breaking with grief. He felt such despair and sorrow that there is a mood of desperation in the story.

Jesus asked for the 'cup' to be taken away from him. The cup stands for suffering and death. The despair and anguish Jesus felt was so deep that the English language cannot properly translate the Greek verbs used in this passage. Verse 33 contains two such verbs that are translated as 'horror' and 'dismay'. The Greek verb translated 'horror' carries the following meanings:

- 'suggestive of shuddering awe';
- 'terrified surprise'; and
- 'amazement amounting to shock'.

The Greek verb translated 'dismay' carries the following meanings:

- 'distress that follows a great shock'; and
- 'agitated'.

The impact of these two verbs together is overwhelming. They convey a feeling of unbounded horror and suffering.

The Crucifixion (14 and 15)

In Mark the only words of Jesus from the cross are the words of extreme anguish:

> Eli, eli, lema sabachthani?
> My God, my God, why hast thou forsaken
> me (15:34).

It is as if Jesus cried, 'Why me?'. These words are the first verse of Psalm 22. Some scholars have suggested that Jesus was beginning to recite the Psalm but died before finishing it. It is more in keeping with the theme of suffering found in Mark's Gospel to suggest that Jesus felt deserted by God in this moment of extreme agony.

Some Christians see in the words of Jesus the close identity Jesus felt with sinners as he was committed into their hands (14:41) as one appointed by God to give his life as a 'ransom for many' (10:45).

One further interpretation is that the words show a belief in God even in the agony of death. It may be that Mark's church preserved the words for that very reason. For a church suffering persecution the idea of a Jesus who still prayed and showed faith in God at the moment of death would be a great comfort in their own distress.

SUMMARY

- Mark builds on the suffering of Jesus which ends in death. Jesus accepts his destiny believing it to be planned by his father, even though it means pain, suffering, humiliation and rejection.
- Through this suffering and death, Mark sees Jesus as the sacrifice for humanity, a sacrifice that reconciles people to God.
- For Mark, death becomes the triumph over suffering and the resurrection becomes the triumph over death.

Why did Jesus Die?

Mark insists that it was *inevitable*. This means that Mark saw the death of Jesus as part of God's plan. God wished it. The evidence for this view is found in the Gospel. The Son of Man *must* suffer (see 8:31; 9:1; 9:31; 10:33).

Jesus died because he accepted this plan and was *obedient* to God. He is the one who willingly sets out to Jerusalem (10:32). Ever since Peter's profession of faith at Caesarea Philippi, Jesus travelled towards Jerusalem. On that journey he makes it plain that this is his destiny (10:32); also 8:31; 9:31; 10:32–34).

The death of Jesus is also due to the *wickedness* of humanity. They refuse to accept him as Messiah. They reject his authority (2:7; 2:20; 3:22; 14:10–11; 14:21).

These are the three main ideas in Mark's view of the death of Jesus. It is in these three ways that Mark tries to answer the question, 'Why did Jesus die?'.

What does the death of Jesus mean for Christians today?

The suffering of Jesus was inevitable

Christians believe that the suffering of Jesus was inevitable. While they see Jesus' suffering as part of the experience all people go through, they believe also that Jesus suffered opposition, rejection, hatred and death because of who he was, what he taught and what he did. They accept that Jesus could have avoided dying on the Cross and that he could have slipped away into obscurity. Christians claim he did not because he was obedient to what he knew God wanted from him. This obedience resulted in death because of the wickedness or sin of humanity.

Reconciliation

Christians believe that God sent Jesus into the world to show people a way back to Himself. This coming back to God is called Reconciliation.

Throughout history there have been different theories about how the death of Jesus reconciles people to God. Some of them are not acceptable to all twentieth century Christians.

(a) **God must be satisfied**. *For some Christians in the Middle Ages and even today, this idea of reconciliation was based on the belief that God was offended by the sins of people. A punishment needed to be given. A debt to God needed to be paid. The only one who could pay such a debt was a perfect person because a sinful person would be unacceptable to God. So God sent his son as the victim who would satisfy God's sense of justice.*

There are Christians today who find such a theory distasteful. They would reject any idea of a God who appears to them to be harsh and cruel or who seemed to want his son to suffer pain and death or who needed to be satisfied by a perfect sacrifice.

(b) **Jesus is a ransom**. *Mark talks about Jesus giving*

...his life as a ranson for many (10:45).

The word 'ransom' seems to indicate that a price was paid to God so that he would free people from sin. Again many Christians find this idea difficult to accept. They do not see why God needs a ransom to be paid in order to allow people to come back to him.

(c) **Jesus gives his life as a ransom**. *This is a different theory to the one above. Many Christians understand the word 'ransom' to mean a 'belonging to God'. They would claim God showed such a great love for people that he even allowed Jesus to die on a cross in order that his love might persuade them to return and belong once more to him.*

Jesus as a sacrifice

At the Last Supper, Jesus said,

> This is my blood, the blood of the covenant, shed for many. . . (14:24).

Christians see this verse as very important in understanding the reasons for the death of Jesus. The 'blood of the covenant' is a reference to the time of Moses in the Old Testament. In those times, an animal was offered in sacrifice to God and its blood was sprinkled over the people as a sign of the one blood or life shared between God and Israel. Many Christians do not see Jesus as a sacrifice in the same way. They do not think of him as a sacrifice offered to God; giving his blood to a demanding Father who is 'out for blood'. They see Jesus giving his blood; giving himself to all people. It is his gift. People are now linked with God in one life, the life of the covenant.

Death and resurrection

Some Christians only see meaning in the death of Jesus if it is linked to the resurrection. Without the resurrection they do not see how the death of Jesus achieves anything. In the light of the resurrection they see that victory has triumphed over death. Just as God freed the slaves from their captivity in Egypt at the time of Moses, so through the death and resurrection of Jesus God frees people from the slavery of sin and death. They see the power of God's love as so strong that it overcomes sin and death. Humanity is now reconciled to God even if some people are unaware of the good news.

Study Skills

Knowledge

1 What did God say at the baptism of Jesus?
2 What was the reaction of the Pharisees to the curing, by Jesus, of the man with the withered hand?
3 What did Jesus say about his coming death in Mark's Gospel?
4 How did the disciples respond to Jesus' predictions?
5 Write out the words of the Institution of the Last Supper.
6 What is the meaning of the sentence, 'Eli, eli, lema sabachthani'?

Understanding

7 'Jesus tried to prepare his disciples for his coming death' Do you think this is a true statement as found in Mark's Gospel? Give reasons and examples in your answer.
8 What do you understand Jesus to mean by the words he spoke on the cross in Mark's account of the Crucifixion?

Evaluation

9 Why do you think Mark places such a lot of emphasis on the suffering and death of Jesus?
10 'The Gospel of Mark is a Passion Narrative with an extended introduction.' Do you think this is a good summary of Mark's Gospel?

Examination Practice

Read the following passage carefully, noting the words in italics and answer the questions below it.

'The hour of the crucifixion was nine in the morning, and the inscription giving the charge against him read, "*The King of the Jews*". Two bandits were crucified with him, one on his right and the other on his left.

The passers-by hurled abuse at him: "Aha!" they cried, wagging their heads, "You would pull the Temple down, would you, and build it in three days? Come down from the cross and save yourself!" So too the chief priests and lawyers jested with one another: "*He saved others*," they said, "*but he cannot save himself*. Let the Messiah, the King of Israel, come down now from the cross. If we see that, we shall believe." Even those who were crucified with him taunted him' (15:25–32).

    (a) Why do you think the inscription 'King of the Jews' was put on the cross? (4)
    (b) Jesus was ridiculed by passers-by, their religious leaders and those crucified with him. Why was this? (4)

(c) 'He saved others'. Illustrate this saying by describing *one* incident when Jesus 'saved' other people during his life. (4)

(d) Mark put great emphasis on the death of Jesus. Explain the reasons for doing this. Why is this death important to Christians?   (8)

Practical Work

• Find out how the different Christian Churches celebrate the last week of Jesus' life. Try to discover the emphasis they place on the Crucifixion. This could be done by either inviting representatives of the Churches into school or by interviewing them outside of school.

9 The Resurrection of Jesus in Mark's Gospel

The purpose of this chapter is to try to discover what it means for Mark to say 'Jesus is risen'. There are two important questions to be discussed.

– What did the resurrection mean to Mark?
– What does the resurrection mean for Christians today?

What did the Resurrection Mean to Mark?

The Empty Tomb (16:1–8)

Mark has the shortest account of the resurrection. He only has one story. It is the story of the empty tomb. He records how Mary of Magdala, Mary, the mother of James, and Salome went to the tomb early on the Sunday morning to anoint the body of Jesus with spices. As they walked along they were discussing how the big stone could be removed from the entrance to the tomb. When they arrived they found the stone had already been rolled away. On going into the tomb they found a young man in white who gave them the message of resurrection.

> Fear nothing; you are looking for Jesus of Nazareth, who was crucified. He has been raised again; he is not here; look, there is the place where they laid him (16:6).

The messenger went on to give them a message for the disciples and especially Peter:

> He is going on before you into Galilee; there you will see him, as he told you (16:7).

The women ran away from the tomb. They were terrified. They did not tell anybody what they had seen or heard. Mark's Gospel finishes at this point.

The main teaching of this story of the empty tomb is found

in the words of the messenger. It is a teaching that is expressed simply yet, for Christians, is at the very centre of their faith. Jesus is risen. He had died on the cross on Friday but now he has risen from the dead.

The Problem of the Ending of Mark's Gospel

Even though Mark expresses simply the message of resurrection the story of the empty tomb does present problems. It is a very strange ending. Not only does the Gospel end on a note of fear and despair but Mark does not record one single resurrection appearance.

For a long time it has been thought that Mark's Gospel was incomplete. When it is compared with the Gospels of Matthew and Luke, Mark's appears unfinished as both the others have resurrection appearances.

Three Different Endings

It is obvious that the early Christians also thought the Gospel was unfinished for in later copies of Mark's Gospel three different endings can be found, each of which has been added by somebody else.

The Canonical Ending
In most New Testaments there can be found what is known as the canonical ending (16:9–20). This ending probably comes from the second century and is obviously a summary of the resurrection stories found in the other Gospels.

This ending can be divided into four parts:

(a) **The appearance to Mary of Magdala** (16:9–11). Jesus appears to Mary of Magdala from whom seven devils had been cast out (see Luke 8:2). The story is a summary of the appearance to Mary found in John's Gospel (John 20:11–18).

(b) **The appearance to two travellers** (16:12–13). Jesus appears in a disguised form to two of the disciples 'on their way into the country'. This is an obvious reference to the Emmaus Road narrative in Luke where Jesus appeared to Cleopas and his companion and talked with them as they walked along (Luke 24:13–35).

(c) **The appearance to the eleven** (16:14–18). This section recalls passages from all three other Gospels (see Luke

24:36–49; John 20:19–23; Matthew 28:16–20). Jesus rebukes the disciples because they had not believed the message of resurrection. Then he commissions them to go into the world and preach the Gospel message.

(d) **The ascension** (16:19–20). The ending is concluded with Jesus being carried up to heaven to be at the right hand of God. His work is now over and the disciples begin their mission confident that Jesus is still with them (Luke 24:50–51).

The Shorter Ending (16:8)
The shorter ending is found in some translations of Mark's Gospel.

'And they delivered all these instructions briefly to Peter and his companions. Afterwards Jesus himself sent out by them from east to west the sacred and imperishable message of eternal salvation.'

The words are not Mark's. The language is obviously different to that of the rest of the Gospel. Nowhere else in the Gospel does Mark use such words as 'sacred'; 'imperishable' or 'salvation'. They are an attempt to finish the Gospel.

The Freer Ending
In one early manuscript dating back to the fifth century there is an additional ending placed after Mark 16:14. It reads:

'And they excused themselves, saying, "This age of lawlessness and disbelief is under Satan, who does not permit the true power of God to prevail over the unclean things of the spirits. Therefore reveal your righteousness now". Thus they addressed Christ, but Christ said to them in reply, "The term of the years of Satan's authority has been fulfilled, but other terrible things draw near, even for the sinners for whom I was handed over in death, that they might return to the truth and sin no more, that they might inherit the spiritual and incorruptible glory of righteousness which is in heaven".'

Again the words are not those of Mark. They have close similarity with ideas expressed by Paul in some of his letters and also the Acts of the Apostles where Luke records the commission given to Paul after his conversion (Acts 26:18).

Two main conclusions can be made about the three endings:

1 they were not written by Mark and form no part of his Gospel; and
2 they were all written because Mark's Gospel was thought to be incomplete.

Is Mark's Gospel Finished?

Various suggestions have been made as to why the Gospel seems unfinished. All of them assume that there must have been more material which has been lost. At first, these suggestions are attractive but all of them can be seriously questioned.

(a) **Was the ending of the Gospel deliberately removed?** It has been suggested that the ending of the Gospel was removed because some people did not like what Mark had written. It is difficult, however, to think of any content that would have called for such drastic action. This idea seems to create more difficulties than it solves.

(b) **Was the Gospel accidentally mutilated?** It has been suggested that the ending of the Gospel was torn by accident. After all, the scrolls were fragile. This is certainly a possibility. It is hard, however, to imagine that a repair would not have been made or that Mark would not have re-written the ending, if he was still alive to do so.

(c) **Did Mark die before he could finish his Gospel?** Again it has been suggested that Mark was killed or died before he had a chance to finish his Gospel. Certainly, it is possible. Arrest or execution was a real possibility in the Rome of Mark's day but it is surely most likely that the manuscript would have been finished off by a disciple of Mark's before being circulated to the churches.

All these suggestions seem empty. Each assumes that there was a lost ending to the Gospel.

There is a further important fact that must be considered. There is no evidence whatsoever that there ever was an ending following on from verse 8. The only text available in the early Church ends with the words 'for they were afraid'. In view of the fact that Mark's Gospel circulated widely throughout the early Christian communities, it is even more surprising that there is no knowledge of any text going beyond 16:8 if, of course, such a text ever existed.

Conclusion on the Ending

1   It may well be that Mark's Gospel is unfinished but this is not proven.
2   The claim that the Gospel is unfinished is based on assumptions, some of which create more difficulties than they solve.
3   It is possible that the Gospel finished with those stark and despairing words, 'they said nothing to anybody, for they were afraid'.

A Second Problem (16:7)

There is a second problem in the story of the empty tomb. The problem concerns the words of the young man in white to Mary of Magdala and her companions.

> But go and give this message to his disciples and Peter: 'He is going on before you to Galilee; there you will see him, as he told you' (16:7).

The problem is easily stated. There seems to be a direct contradiction between verse 7 and verse 8. In verse 7 the message is that the disciples will see Jesus in Galilee. In the next verse the women fail to deliver the message, so disobeying the command. It seems hard to believe that Mark meant such a contradiction. The problem depends on the interpretation of verse 7.

At first glance the impulse is to see this verse as referring to the resurrection but some scholars believe it refers to something else yet to come. This is the Second Coming of Jesus, known as the Parousia.

The ending of the Gospel now makes sense. The phrase, 'there you will see him' refers to the future; a future yet to happen and which cannot be recorded because it has not yet happened.

It is important to realise that Mark records the message of resurrection with the story of the empty tomb. He sees this, however, as a temporary situation before Jesus comes again.

SUMMARY

1   There is no evidence that the Gospel ended in any other way than 'They said nothing to anybody, for they were afraid (16:8). Therefore, it may be that Mark purposely does not include a resurrection appearance.

2   The words 'He is going on before you into Galilee; there you will see him, as he told you' (16:7) could refer to the Second Coming of Jesus and not to a missing resurrection appearance.

3   Perhaps there are no resurrection appearances in Mark because they would be confused with the message of the Second Coming of Jesus. Although the resurrection is announced, it is as if it is taken for granted. Mark's readers already believe that Jesus had risen from the dead. They believe he is with them daily.

4   Mark's readers lived in the time of the resurrection. They suffered persecution in the name of Jesus. They longed for the Second Coming of Jesus when suffering would be no more. Mark writes to encourage them to prepare for that moment when 'they will see the Son of Man coming in the clouds with great power and glory' (13:26).

What does the resurrection mean for Christians today?

There is no historical evidence for the resurrection other than the fact that the disciples believed it happened. Nobody witnessed the actual resurrection itself. Yet the Christian faith stands or falls with the resurrection. As Paul says in his first letter to the Church at Corinth:

'If there be no resurrection, then Christ was not raised; and if Christ was not raised, then our gospel is null and void, and so is your faith. . .' (1 Corinthians 15:13).

What about the empty tomb?

The only story Mark records about the resurrection is the account of the empty tomb. It is freely accepted by Christians that the fact of the empty tomb proves nothing in itself. The question of the empty tomb has been surrounded by argument since the early days of Christianity. Many theories have been put forward from time to time, to try to explain why the tomb was empty:

1   Jesus was not really dead when he was put in the tomb; he was only in a coma and later revived in the cool of the tomb;
2   the women went to the wrong tomb on the first Easter day; and
3   someone stole the body of Jesus. There are only three groups of people who could have done such a thing: the disciples; the Jewish leaders; or the Roman authorities.

The only trouble with these different theories is, that even for a lot of non-Christians, they make little sense. It is difficult to imagine anyone being able to survive death by crucifixion. Even if it were possible there is no answer given to the question of what happened to Jesus afterwards. Again, if the women had gone to the wrong tomb it is highly unlikely that someone would not have checked when the rumours of resurrection began to circulate. Finally, there seems no reason why anyone would have stolen the body of Jesus. If the disciples stole the body then Christianity is based on a lie. It is difficult to accept that the disciples would live this lie to the extent of even dying for their so-called faith in resurrection. If either the Romans or the Jewish leaders had stolen the body, why did they not produce the evidence when the disciples began to preach that Jesus was risen from the dead?

Such theories do not trouble Christians today not just because they do not believe them, but because their faith is not based simply on the empty tomb. They believe in the resurrection. The story of the empty tomb is secondary. It is, for Christians, the resurrection that matters. It is the resurrection that makes sense of the empty tomb and not the empty tomb that proves the resurrection.

Did the resurrection happen?

Christians believe that something happened after the death of Jesus. They believe this not just because the tomb was empty or that there are in the other Gospels, stories of Jesus appearing to the disciples. There is another reason. The existence of the Christian Church is based on the resurrection. Something happened after the resurrection to transform the disciples from hopeless, frightened and disappointed men, who had deserted

Jesus and run away, into men of courage, who spoke boldly in public, who were no longer frightened and who were prepared to die for what they believed. The disciples themselves gave the reason for this change of attitude. They were convinced that Jesus was alive. In the Acts of the Apostles, which records the beginnings of the Church, everytime the disciples preached, the message was the same: 'the Jesus we speak of has been raised by God, as we can all bear witness' (Acts 2:32) (see also Acts 3:26; 4:10; 5:31; 10:40; 13:30; 17:31).

It would seem that the existence of the Christian Church is due to the conviction that Jesus had risen from the dead.

What happened?

It is impossible to say what happened at the moment of the resurrection as there were no witnesses. Therefore it is understandable that Christian viewpoints differ over what actually happened.

Some Christians have suggested that the resurrection did not happen at all. They claim that the disciples became aware of who Jesus was and what he had come to do only after his death and were inspired to carry on his work. This has happened throughout history. Many people, for example, devoted themselves to the cause of civil rights in America after the assassination of Martin Luther King in 1968. They were inspired by his leadership and his beliefs. The main difficulty with this view is that it ignores the accounts of the empty tomb and the resurrection appearances and does not satisfactorily explain the extraordinary change that came over the disciples. It is difficult to see how they suddenly came to believe in resurrection, express it in the way they did and begin the process of building Christianity on what, after all, was an untruth.

Others believe that Jesus rose from the dead in bodily form. They point out that the stories of resurrection speak of Jesus being touched, talking and eating (John 20:27; Luke 24:41–43; John 21:15–22). They see a firm link between the Jesus who had lived with them and the risen Lord. Jesus was dead but had been brought back to life. The main weakness with this point of view is that it ignores some of the evidence of the Gospels. It oversimplifies the mystery of the resurrection and reduces it to a corpse coming back to life.

A third view accepts the bodily resurrection of Jesus but also allows for other matters to be taken into consideration. The resurrection was not just a corpse coming back to life. There was *something different about Jesus after the resurrection. The disciples, for example, sometimes did not recognise him (Luke 24:16). Some doubted that it was Jesus (Matthew 28:17; Luke 24:42). Jesus seemed to be able to come and go in a manner that was not normal (Luke 24:31; John 20:19, 26). Above all he is recognised, accepted and worshipped in faith. Even for the first Christians, faith was the only way to a full understanding of the risen Christ.*

What does the resurrection mean?

(a) Christians believe the resurrection proves the identity of Jesus. Jesus is, without doubt, the Christ (Messiah) of God. He is the Son of Man, the Son of God, the Lord (see chapter 2). A Christian is one who confesses that Jesus is Lord.

(b) Christians believe the resurrection confirms the work of Jesus. His life and death were an attempt to bring all people back to God. God has confirmed that work in raising Jesus from the dead. Through the resurrection, forgiveness of sins can take place and people can be restored to God.

(c) Christians believe that the resurrection means something in everyday experience. It is not simply an event in the past but has meaning for the present. They believe Jesus is alive and with them day by day.

(d) Christians believe that the resurrection means that death has been overcome. Jesus has triumphed over death. For his followers death is not the end but the beginning of eternal life that already exists in the relationship enjoyed with the risen Jesus here and now.

Study Skills

Knowledge

1 Who went to the tomb early on the Sunday morning?
2 Why did they go to the tomb?
3 Who gave them the message that Jesus had risen from the dead?
4 What was the message for Peter and the disciples?
5 How does Mark's Gospel end (16:8)?
6 How many different endings are there to Mark's Gospel beyond 16:8?

Understanding

7 What do you understand to be the problem with the ending of Mark's Gospel?
8 Explain the words 'He is going on before you into Galilee; there you will see him. . .'.

Evaluation

9 How important do you think belief in the empty tomb is to an understanding of resurrection?
10 Explain one difficulty a person might have in believing the resurrection. How would you answer that difficulty?

Examination Practice

Give a careful account of Mark's story of the empty tomb.   (6)
Why do you think the women failed to deliver the message of resurrection to the disciples?   (5)
Outline briefly the other story where Jesus teaches about resurrection in Mark's Gospel.   (4)
What do Christians believe about the resurrection?   (5)

Practical Work

• In small groups, work out three simple questions on the resurrection. Each member of the group should then interview one or two adult Christians on the basis of the three questions. Then, in the groups, compile the results of this survey into belief in the resurrection.

10 The Future

The purpose of this chapter is to discover the meaning of the teaching of the Gospel about the Second Coming of Jesus. This can be done by examining the following.

– What is apocalyptic writing?
– An analysis of the chapter.
– What does the teaching of the Second Coming of the Son of Man mean for Christians today?

What is Apocalyptic Writing?

(a) Chapter 13 is unusual in that it is the only time in Mark's Gospel when Jesus delivers a long speech (called a discourse).

(b) It is written in the style of what is known as 'apocalyptic literature'. The Greek word 'apocalypse' means 'unveiling' or 'revealing a secret'.

(c) The title 'apocalyptic' was used for writings that spoke about the future, not in the sense of prophecy, but in the sense of events in the future that only God could know and was prepared to 'reveal'.

(d) Such writing is in a disguised form, often using highly symbolic and 'word picture' language.

(e) Such writing has its origin in Jewish history. The prophets of old looked upon God as the sovereign Lord of all creation. He controlled all the events of the world. His purpose would be fulfilled in history. This history would reach a climax when God established his kingdom over the whole world. The idea of this coming event of God's final rule over all things is called 'eschatology' (literally, 'at the end').

(f) Later on in Jewish history, in the second century BC, the Jews suffered the humiliation of defeat at the hands of the Greeks. The belief that God would still bring about his final rule over the whole of mankind took on a new significance. The ideas about the end of the world began to be written in terms of catastrophe. God would bring about the end in a violent and devastating way. The wicked would come to an end and God would rule supreme surrounded by the good. This type of writing was called 'apocalyptic'.

(g) The language of apocalyptic writing is very vivid. It is full of supernatural wonder, angels and visions of good and evil.

(h) Apocalyptic writing normally arose at times of great suffering or persecution. Its aim was to encourage the faithful. The best example of apocalyptic writing in the Old Testament is the book of Daniel. The New Testament contains the apocalyptic book of Revelation.

(i) Mark's chapter 13 is an example of Christian apocalyptic writing.

An Analysis of the Chapter

The main problem with the apocalyptic chapter of Mark's Gospel is that it seems to be dealing with two distinct themes:

1   the Second Coming of the Son of Man; and
2   the fall of Jerusalem in 70 AD.

It has been suggested that the chapter is a combination of two different sources. It contains the teaching of Jesus about the events of destruction that were to happen when the Romans sacked Jerusalem. Into this teaching Mark has inserted a second source of material from Christian apocalyptic writing about the end of the world. It has been suggested that this apocalyptic writing (called the 'Little Apocalypse') may be found in verses 7–8; 14–20; 24–27.

The whole chapter has been worked over by Mark so much that it is virtually impossible to distinguish his meaning. One thing is certain. Mark is writing to encourage his readers who were undergoing great persecution. He tells them to be faithful and forecasts the signs that are to herald the end and which are to free them from their misery and see the glorious return of Jesus.

13:1–4
The discourse is introduced by a discussion about the Temple. As Jesus and his disciples were leaving the Temple one day during the final week, one of the disciples commented on its magnificence. This was the Temple of Herod the Great, begun in 20 BC (see chapter 1).

Jesus, aware that the Jews' relationships with their Roman masters would finally lead to disaster, forecasts that the Temple will be destroyed. This was to happen in 70 AD, six

years after the building was completed. Later on, sitting with
Jesus on the slope of the Mount of Olives, overlooking the
Temple, Peter, with Andrew, James and John, asks Jesus
when this destruction of the Temple is to take place.

Their question does not seem to receive an answer for
Mark uses this conversation as an introduction to the more
general apocalyptic teaching which he wants to put over to
his readers. It has been suggested that Jesus' answer to this
question of the disciples is found later in the discourse when
he says,

> I tell you this: the present generation will live to see
> it all *(13:30)*.

13:5–6; 9–13
These verses contain warnings given to the disciples. They
are probably based on what Jesus said on other occasions but
have been gathered together by Mark. They have also been
adapted by Mark to fit in with the experiences of his readers.
The teaching in the verses is clear.

(a) Disciples must beware of false Messiahs (13:3–6).

(b) They must be on their guard for they were to undergo
arrest, flogging and appearances in court. This was already
the experience of many of Mark's readers. They were not to
be overawed by such experiences for the Holy Spirit would
give them courage and strength.

They must also be on their guard against betrayal. To be a
Christian would bring hatred and would split families.
Again, this was already the experience of many early
Christians. By the time Mark wrote his Gospel the great
persecution of Christians had taken place in Rome. Beginning
in 64 AD the Emperor Nero had thousands of Christians
persecuted and killed. It was in these persecutions that,
according to Christian tradition both Peter and Paul died.

13:7–8
This is the first part of the Little Apocalypse. The language is
typical in its emphasis on war, earthquakes and famines. It is
claimed that these are the signs of a new age which will
precede the end.

13:14–20
This passage, which is part of the Little Apocalypse, begins
with a reference to 'the Abomination of Desolation' (13:14).

This is a phrase from the Old Testament which means 'an appalling sacrilege'.

Originally, in the book of Daniel, the phrase referred to a statue of Zeus, the Greek God, which was set up in the Temple at Jerusalem in 168 BC by the ruler Antiochus Epiphanies. The kingdom ruled over by Antiochus included Palestine, and he was insistent that the Jews followed the Greek religion. He even had pigs sacrified on the altar of the Temple. This was sacrilege and it led to a rebellion against Antiochus. Obviously Mark intends his readers to think of a horror, yet to come, which would be just as offensive. Two such occasions have been suggested.

(a) Mark may have in mind the attempt made by the Emperor Caligula to set up his own statue in the Temple in 40 AD. He had declared himself a god. The Jews were finally spared this indignity because Caligula died before his orders could be carried out. But it is doubtful whether Mark was referring to this event as it had already happened by the time he wrote his Gospel.

(b) It is much more likely that Mark was referring to the destruction of Jerusalem and its Temple in 70 AD. Most probably Mark was writing during the preceding rebellion 65 AD and he used this vague language to warn of the impending disaster. Certainly the warning reflects the idea of approaching armies and the fleeing population. The passage ends with the promise that this coming time of distress will be short (13:19–20).

13:21–23
These verses enlarge on the theme already mentioned in 13:5–6, which warned that there would be false Christs and prophets.

13:24–27
This is the final part of the Little Apocalypse and is typical in its language. The end of the world is to be preceded by cosmic disorder. Mark intends his readers to think of the time when all Christians will be gathered together by the Son of Man when he returns. The verse which makes reference to the Son of Man is a quotation from the apocalyptic book of Daniel (Daniel 7:13–14), but Mark intends it to relate to Jesus' Second Coming.

13:28–32
Mark goes on to include a parable dealing with the time of the end. The fig tree breaking into leaf heralds the approach of summer. In the same way all these signs herald the time of the end.

In verse 30 Mark says that 'the present generation will live to see it all'. This is in direct contrast with verse 32,

> But about that day or that hour no one knows, not even the angels in heaven, not even the Son; only the Father.

One way of resolving this contradiction is to suggest that verse 30 refers to the destruction of Jerusalem and that verse 32 refers to the end of the world. It is interesting to note that Jesus states that he does not know when it will happen. This tends to discredit those attempts in history to forecast the event and pours scorn on those today who constantly and confidently predict the end of the world.

13:33–37
The discourse ends with a command to be alert. Mark is saying that when the end comes it will be sudden, in spite of all the signs. It is the task of the Christian to be alert and watchful.

SUMMARY

- The apocalyptic chapter covers two subjects:

1   the fall of Jerusalem; and
2   the coming of the Son of Man at the end of the world.

- False prophets will appear. Persecution of Christians will take place.
- The Abomination of Desolation will be set up. Jerusalem will be destroyed.
- The signs of the end of the world will be found in the heavens and the Son of Man will return to gather the faithful.
- No one knows when this will happen.
- The duty of the Christian is to be alert, for the end will come suddenly.

What does the teaching of the Second Coming of the Son of Man mean for Christians today?

In the Old Testament the belief developed that the Son of Man would come to his own people and establish the rule of God on earth. This was carried forward into the Christian era. Christians today still believe that Jesus will return.

(a) Some Christians see the coming of Jesus, born in Bethlehem, as the coming of the Son of Man. They believe that God has visited his people and in the life, death and resurrection of Jesus, the new era of God's kingdom can be seen.

(b) Others believe that Jesus' resurrection is to be seen as his return in glory.

(c) Still others believe, as the early Church did, that there will be a time in the future when Jesus, as Son of Man, will come again. At that time he will establish God's kingdom for all to see. It will be undeniable and unmistakable.

(d) Mark's Gospel comments on this in two different ways: no one knows when it will happen; and Christians must be alert and ready for it.

(e) Most Christians would say that the language used to describe this future event is symbolic. It is not to be taken literally. What the language is attempting to say is that Jesus will return and when he does it will be an unmistakable happening. Everybody will witness it.

(f) The teaching of Mark should be sufficient for people to realise that the timing of the Second Coming is not known. Yet throughout history, certain groups of people have, from time to time, discredited the teaching of the Second Coming through misuse of the Bible. Using involved and futile calculations they have attempted to predict the moment when Jesus will return. Such activity is, at best, useless; at worst, it places Christianity in a position of ridicule.

Study Skills

Knowledge

1   Which building were the disciples talking about when they commented on its greatness?

2   Who asked Jesus when the destruction of this building would take place?
3   What does the word 'apocalypse' mean?
4   Jesus warns his disciples to be on their guard. Name three things which he says will happen to them.
5   What was the original 'Abomination of Desolation'?
6   Name the three heavenly 'signs' that will precede the Coming of the Son of Man.

Understanding

7   What possible interpretations can there be for Mark's use of the phrase 'Abomination of Desolation'?
8   What do you understand to be the theme or themes of the apocalyptic chapter of Mark's Gospel? Give examples from the chapter in your answer.

Evaluation

9   What do you think Mark means by the return of the Son of Man? How do you think Christians interpret the signs of that Coming as outlined in Mark's Gospel?

Practical Work

•   Write a poem or draw a picture that shows Mark's vision of the future as found in the apocalyptic discourse.

Index of Markan References